HEAR MY HEARTBEAT:
The Story of Enduring Love

Jenny Rebecca Haust

PRAISE FOR

HEAR MY HEARTBEAT
by Jenny Haust

Hear My Heartbeat is an incredible story that those who have experienced pregnancy loss can deeply relate to. For those who have not, this story serves as an emotional guide through the unfathomable depths of grief. Jenny beautifully and bravely shares her experience through the pain of losing her baby while simultaneously honoring her grief and the life she's built since.

- Melanie Jennings, LMHC

ISBN: ISBN 979-8-218-48999-1

Printed in the United States of America

TriFaith Publishing

First Edition-2024

Cover design by Ella Smith

For my daughter Jenny

Table of Contents

Foreword

When I was a child, I never gave much thought to life as a grown-up. I was just enjoying being a little girl. But I did grow up, a child of the 1980s, and all the things that happened along the way brought me through the usual challenges and joys of school, friendships, jobs, and romances.

I married my husband, Steve, in October 1999. We had fallen in love a few years earlier and dreamed of making it official by tying the knot. We knew we wanted children someday; however, we both were wrapped up with our careers and wanted to enjoy just being newlyweds for a while. We worked hard, traveled, and simply enjoyed the early days of our marriage.

In 2002, we made the decision to start a family. *Hear My Heartbeat* evolved from this decision. I never could have imagined my journey to motherhood would have taken me on the arduous path it did. It is through this journey that I have been taught invaluable lessons about life, love, and persistence. I struggled as I had never done before. At times, I still struggle. I have been fortunate to find and discover a strength and gratitude within myself that I may never have uncovered had I not taken this journey. These lessons sustain me and ground me. Each day, I wake with gratitude for my family and friends. Most importantly, I am grateful to be called "Mom" or "Momma" by my two sons,

Ethan and Erich. They have made it possible for me to experience motherhood, which has been the greatest gift of my life.

I began writing this story in 2010, but I was not ready. At times, it feels like the passing of all the years has made things easier but then each December the sorrow comes rushing back. I still have difficulty talking openly about my experience. I believe I always will. This book is not meant to fill your heart with sadness. Quite simply, I have chosen to write about my experiences in the hope that my story might be of comfort to other women who have endured similar losses and that it will serve as a reflection upon the privilege I have known in becoming a mother. It is a great responsibility, but it is also the greatest blessing that has been bestowed upon me.

I thank my family and friends for their love and support. My mom and dad have walked with me all these years with love, compassion, and the silent understanding of my struggle. I couldn't have written this without Linda Loomis. Her belief in my telling this story and encouraging me each step of the way have helped me produce this book. Most importantly, I thank the Lord for my baby girl Jenny and my two wonderful sons.

October 2010

"Mom, where are you?"

I sense the urgency in six-year-old Ethan's voice.

"I'm up in my closet! Put your sneakers and your coat on now or you'll miss the bus," I yell back. "I'll be right down."

It's Monday morning. I'm in a hurry. The kids and I had a tough time getting up and out of bed on this dreary autumn morning. It's rainy and dark. I'm throwing my clothes on as I don't have time to shower.

"Put your backpack on, please. I promise I'm coming down!" I yell.

Today, I'm filling in for one of Erich's nursery school teachers who had fallen ill over the weekend. Janet, the director, called this morning and asked if I could help at the last minute.

"Mom, are you coming?"

"Yes," I yell again. "Yes!"

I need a coat. I close the white door to my small walk-in closet. The closet light is a flush mount on the ceiling. It has never been bright enough to really get a good look at exactly what is hanging in my closet. I don't know if the light bulb is not the correct wattage or if the thick white coating on the glass cover keeps the light from really shining through. I have clothes hanging everywhere along with jeans and sweaters folded on the shelves. I installed a copycat California Closet organization system years ago. It hasn't helped. Everything is mixed together except for my coats. There is no sense of organization here, just clothing chaos. At the very least, I know all coats are located to the left through the narrow doorway.

I must actually walk through the slim door entrance and shut the door behind me to be able to see the coats located behind it. It's tight. I need to choose a coat of some type, and I need to choose one fast. It is unseasonably warm today. I don't want anything heavy as I know I'll sweat. I'm always sweating, even under minimal heat. I'll choose a vest that can withstand the rain while allowing my body to still breathe. I flip through the hangers on the metal rod one by one looking for something to match my cream-colored, long-sleeve cotton shirt.

I come to my pink fleece hooded jacket. I stop and stare closely at it. It stands out from my inventory of gray and black outerwear. It seems I inherited my maternal grandmother's love of these two non-colors. But there, between a long black, wool winter coat and a gray puffer jacket is my bright, cheerful pink fleece. A happy color. The color of Bubble Yum gum from my days as a child or the color of a beautiful pink flamingo. It has a solid black zipper along with matching hood ties. The front looks worn, with fleece pilled from all the wear. I swallow. I slide the hanger to look at the next coat and the jacket falls off the hanger onto the floor. I bend down to pick it up and put it back on the hanger. Touching the jacket, I instantly travel back in time. The fleece feels cozy in my hands. I can't help but hold the coat close to me. I put it to my nose to see if it still has the scent I vividly remember. I take a deep breath and realize the scent has faded. I pull it away from my nose and stare at it. I am reminded of what this jacket represents. I close my eyes. A flood of emotions fills me.

"Mom, I am going to miss the bus!" Ethan yells.

I quickly put the jacket on the hanger and place it back where I found it. I grab the gray vest next to it and run down the stairs to get Ethan out the door and to the bus stop across the street.

December 2000

I recall the excitement Steve and I shared when we closed on our very first home. We were thrilled. We had completed the move from Boston to Syracuse. I was happy my company was gracious enough to transfer me and grant me a promotion at the same time. My hard work was paying off. Steve settled into his new position and I into mine. The days came and went as we focused on our careers and performed all the duties of homeowners. I wanted to fill the house with more than just furniture; however, I knew it wasn't yet time to bring a baby into our world. But I thought we had space in our hearts and home for new life.

"I really want a dog," I said to Steve.

He turned to me with a surprised expression and asked what kind of dog I had in mind.

"I would really love to have a beagle," I said, with sweet memories of my childhood pet.

"Well, if we get a dog, I really want a large breed," he replied.

After some debate, we settled on looking for a beagle to join us in our new house. We were adamant that we wanted a dog from a responsible breeder who loved animals, not someone who just kept dogs to make money. I began making inquiries.

"You're not a puppy mill?" I asked the gentleman at the other end of the phone.

"No, ma'am," responded a deep voice.

I asked if my husband and I could visit and look at puppies on the weekend. He said yes. So on a golden autumn Saturday, we headed east a few hours out of Syracuse to look for a beagle puppy who would share our love.

"Lord, this is far off the beaten path," I said to Steve.

"No kidding."

We left the main road as we turned right onto a long unpaved drive. The path led us up a small hill into a wooded area. We came to a large brushed-silver metal gate, the kind farmers use to contain livestock. We pulled up close to it, put the car in park and got out.

"Are we in the right place?" Steve asked.

"I have no idea."

There was no mailbox or any form of identification to indicate where we actually were. I could see a small brown cabin nestled in the distance. Leaves of fall colors covered the ground as we walked along in the sunshine bucking a heavy wind. I stared through the gate, I gasped at what was coming toward us. All I could think of was the scene from *101 Dalmatians.* In the distance, I witnessed what looked to be 101 beagle puppies running our way. I couldn't believe it. I had never seen so many puppies. Tails wagging and full of excitement, they were headed to the gate entrance. Despite how sweet and cute they were, I was pissed. We had been deceived. This was a puppy mill.

"We are not getting a dog here," Steve grumbled.

"I can't leave a puppy here in this hell hole!" I exclaimed, thinking that if we could rescue even one, it would be merciful.

We proceeded carefully through the gate so as not to let any of the puppies out and continued up toward the small brown cabin. As we walked, the puppies all scattered about like twisting schools of fish in the ocean. One brown eyed, floppy eared pup was cuter than the next. They were running in packs, wrestling with one another. They appeared happy and free. I could see an older dog chained to the tree in the distance. My heart sank. A large unkempt man stepped out of the brown cabin. He called to us in a raspy, smoker's voice. I felt uncomfortable and angry. To my right, a large maple tree, full of yellow leaves that had not yet fallen off, cast a beautiful glow from the sun shining through from above. In front of the tree sat a small, little tri-colored beagle puppy all by itself. It appeared that all the other puppies were playing together, and this one sat alone. I walked over, bent down, and picked up the puppy.

“Are you not being included?” I asked.

Happy to have my attention, the puppy wiggled in excitement and kissed my face. I knew at that very moment this was the little one we would take home. We asked the cost, and listened impatiently as the gruff man explained his fee.

After handing him cash, we walked back toward the gate. I felt guilty leaving all those puppies behind. I felt especially sad for the older dog chained to the tree. How cruel, I thought; how awful. She was only used for breeding. I snuggled our puppy close and kept walking; I could not look back again. Steve got in the driver's seat and I, holding the new member of our family, in the passenger seat. I placed her on my lap and hugged her. Steve and I talked softly as we drove along; we felt we had saved her from a dreary life. We drove back down the dirt path and got onto the main road that led to the highway.

On that sunny autumn afternoon, in the middle of nowhere, we welcomed our beagle, Maude Lilly, into our hearts. Little did I know the role she would play in my life over the next 16 years. Although we had rescued a puppy, it would turn out that in time, she would rescue me.

Baby Haust

Since childhood, I have had a strong inner sense of understanding things unspoken or unconfirmed. I'm not sure what to call it. It is an energy that arouses my senses and guides my feelings. "Intuition" may describe it best. On many occasions while at work or through simple casual interactions, I have been able to sense a certain energy from people. For example, if I shake someone's hand upon introduction, I typically receive some sense of that person's energy from it. Good, bad, or neutral, I get a reading. There were some moments in life when I received negative energy upon that introductory handshake or hello that it frightened me. A strong sense of self accompanied these feelings because I trusted this gift as one way of knowing, or of understanding, my world.

So, when I woke up one spring morning feeling a little off, I knew I was pregnant, even though I was shy of actually being able to confirm this hunch by a few days. I headed to the closest drug store a few days later to buy several pregnancy tests. Once home, I tore the wrapper off the first one and peed on the stick, according to the instructions. Waiting a few minutes as my heart beat faster than normal and staring at this white plastic stick window without much of a blink, I watched as a very faint line appeared. Maybe it was a bit early to know for sure, I thought. I waited a few more days to test again and see if my inner hunch was indeed right.

I followed the same process a few days later. This time, I smiled as a clear red line appeared. Just to be sure, I repeated the test. Same clear red line. I couldn't believe it. Getting pregnant came so easy. I waited for Steve to come home from work to surprise him by handing him the two tests. Steve gave me his brightest smile, but I cautioned him that it was still a bit early. Still, it looked as though our hopes had come true.

"Steve, I want to be certain, so I will take another test tomorrow morning before calling the doctor," I said. I was trying to be practical, but there was no way I could hide the fact that I was giddy with excitement.

The next morning, eager to confirm the positive home tests, I repeated the process just to be sure. Then I called Dr. Randolph's office and set up an appointment to confirm if indeed I was pregnant.

At that first prenatal appointment, I learned that my intuition had been right. And so, the journey began and all the hopes and dreams of becoming a mom were becoming reality. Visions of how life would be with a baby filled my imagination. Wanting to remember each step of the journey, I found a pale green notebook in the drawer next to my desk and decided to keep a simple account of the days, weeks, and months to follow. Although I knew I wouldn't have time to create any in-depth entries, I felt that something on paper would start a record that would someday let this child I was carrying know how very loved and longed for he or she was. And even a brief entry on most days of the pregnancy would be better than nothing, I reasoned.

Now, all these years later, when my heart feels heavy, I pull this pale green notebook out from storage and gaze at the lined pages that are filled with my handwriting. I had used a plain black marker to write the simple title on the cover: "Baby Haust." Reading those journal entries now, I am transported back to a time when a child was growing in my womb and I was full of a mixture of apprehension, hope, and optimism, longing for a successful pregnancy and yearning for a healthy baby.

September 22, 2002

This is my first entry to you baby Haust. I am 11 weeks & 3 days pregnant with you. Boy, have I been sick. I'm nauseous. I decided to wait to start my journal for reasons you will someday understand. Back in January of this year, your daddy and I found out I was pregnant. At one of our checkups, we were so saddened to find out I had miscarried at 7 weeks. After much sadness, we decided to move forward and try once again. July was our lucky month. I knew I was pregnant after just a couple of weeks. It must have been instinct. I found out you were coming at the end of July right before we headed on vacation to Ogunquit, ME and Nantucket, MA. The entire trip was tough. The nausea and fatigue I felt was overwhelming. I kept telling myself this was a good sign you were growing just fine.

Here I am today, relieved, grateful and feeling blessed to have come this far. It has been very worrisome for me. You're doing great so far, and I thank God every night and ask him for continued good luck and health. May he hear my prayers.

I hope you will know how loved you are even at this very moment. No one is more excited about you than me. I will be so blessed by you and God when you finally come into this world. Dr. Randolph said to expect you around April 9th, 2003.

I can't wait! There are so many things to write and say. Hopefully, over the next six months I can fill this journal with lots of info for you. I'm trying not to get too ahead of myself. Tomorrow is another doctor's appointment at 9:00 am. I hope it will go well. I worry.

September 23, 2002

My doctor's visit went well. I could hear your heartbeat on the Doppler. 160-165 beats per minute. Pretty fast, Dr. Randolph said. I fell asleep last night before I took my anti-nausea medicine and awoke this morning vomiting. A good sign, I tell myself, that you are growing and healthy. I will head back to the doctor's in two weeks. I will continue to pray for you.

September 27, 2002

I had to go back to the doctor yesterday. I was having some bad stomach pains and they wanted to make sure all was well with you. Thank God all is good. I heard your heartbeat again 150 beats/minute. The best part was we got to see you on the sonogram. It was amazing. You were lounging in my belly with 1 arm up in the air. Your daddy couldn't believe how much you had grown in 4 and ½ weeks. I couldn't either. It's amazing. Yesterday, we hit the 12-week mark which is huge. My belly has popped out and I'm starting to look like I am pregnant. Your dad says I have "the glow" and said I look beautiful. I keep thinking about what is going on in this belly of mine. You are a miracle for sure. I'm still feeling nauseous even with the medication. You're doing a number on me. Hopefully, in the next week I can get over the hump or turn the corner so many women speak of. I want to get off this medicine. I think by doing so, I will surely feel better.

September 29, 2002

I'm here sitting in bed readying myself for my first day back at work since the end of August. I decided to take the family medical leave act until I could get through this sickness. My boss keeps giving me a hard time when I call in sick or need to come home early due to not feeling well. Yesterday was a rough day as I had some stomach problems. Today, I feel good, except for being exhausted. I'm going to try and take it easy until I can get over the hump. I hope you are comfortable in my belly. I sure hope by going back to work I will not put you in any stress. If so, I will have to think about leaving the job.

October 2, 2002

Today is your dad and my third anniversary. He brought me a dozen red roses. I had another trip to the doctor's today as I had to call in sick to work. Everything looks good and I finally gained some weight. I heard your heartbeat and it sounded strong. Lori, the nurse, was talking to you when we listened to your heartbeat. She said, "you little bugger, you're making your mom really sick." It's all worth it though. I keep dreaming of April when I will finally meet you.

October 8, 2002

It's been almost a week since my last entry. I still am not feeling well and am still on the anti-nausea medicine. I want to be off this drug. If I go off the drugs the vomiting returns, which is not good for you. So I will keep on plugging away. I still am waiting to turn the corner here. When will it come? I feel like I am crawling through these days. The other night, I had a dream that you were a boy. We named you Max, but I kept saying you didn't look like a Max. Then I woke up. So now I'm thinking about what we would name you if you are a boy. I hope with my next entry I can feel better and be off the medicine. That would put me more at ease.

October 15, 2002

Yesterday we went to the doctor. I heard your heartbeat again. It was a strong 150. I'm still so sick and still waiting for it to subside. I'm back working full time and it's been rough. I look forward to April as you will finally be here. I promise to always protect and love you. You will surely be a miracle to me and I will be grateful. Is it April yet?

October 26, 2002

Yesterday was a big day. Dr. Randolph sent me for my 16 week sonogram. At 12:15 p.m. on October 25th there you were. Wow you have grown over the past 2 months. Everything looked great! I saw your heart, your valves and your brain. All I could think was what a miracle you are. We couldn't tell if you were a boy or a girl. Daddy and I agreed we wanted it to be a surprise. I really think a new baby deserves its moment when it comes into this world. So you will have your special moment. I keep thinking about April. I'm focused. Here it is only the end of October. Tonight, we turn the clocks back an hour and winter hasn't even officially arrived, but all my mind imagines is the day you arrive and I can hold you. I said farewell earlier today to the geese as I looked up in the sky as they flew south. My thoughts turned to their return in spring.

We haven't decided what your name will be if you are a boy. If you are a girl, we may name you Ella Catherine. Ella we like because it means beautiful fairy and we (your dad and I) really love that name. Catherine is after my maternal grandmother Miriam Catherine Phillips. She was a beautiful, kind, loving woman and so loved by me. I wish so much she could be here to see you when you arrive. I know she will be in spirit as she had always promised.

And if you are a boy, at this point, we don't have a name for you. In time we will decide. I have to just keep praying and hoping all will continue to go well.

November 5, 2002

You are growing like crazy. I can tell as I feel you flutter every now and then in my belly. I've been still having rough days with a few good ones thrown in. The past few days have not gone well. I'm trying not to worry as I know you are busy growing inside. I'm so excited about you and the days to come. I keep wondering if you are a boy or a girl. I just don't know. Whatever you will be, it is God's will, and I will be happy. I pray you stay healthy, strong, and we can make it to April without any problems. I just keep praying.

November 2002

Another beautiful fall season in Upstate NY was upon us. At work, November was always that final push before the holiday season began to meet my end-of-year sales goals. At the same time, I was busy looking ahead to 2003 with a fresh set of goals and objectives to plan for. I had been in and out of work. I stood in my office next to a large white board figuring how to best tackle the remainder of the work year to get as close as possible to achieving my goals or, even better, exceeding them. I was also focused on creating my first quarter plan for the next year. But I was frustrated because with the constant nausea and exhaustion that accompanied my pregnancy, I didn't have my typical high energy level.

One autumn day, I heard the distant call of geese flying south for the winter. As I looked out the window of my home office, I saw large flocks in the clear blue sky. The honking pulled me out of the house onto my front stoop. Each time I looked up at those migrating geese, I caressed the baby inside my body and thought how different my life would be upon their return. I imagined hearing their call in early April and pictured myself standing outside again, holding my beautiful new baby in my arms.

Autumn passed and I struggled to maintain normal activities despite the nausea and fatigue that challenged me, but never tempered the joy of my anticipation. I found it hard to do anything for the holidays. Thanksgiving was upon us and by then I would usually have all my Christmas decorations up, including my exterior holiday lights. Steve and I had created a tradition of turning on our exterior lights for the season as soon as we had finished our family Thanksgiving dinner. This year, however, instead of having everything ready, I had failed to get all the decorating done. Each time I would drag out the bins and start to string lights, I ended up sitting on the couch to rest instead. Frustrated, I decided to take the decorating slowly, accepting help from my mom and Steve, who ultimately finished the job.

Thanks to them, after we had enjoyed a traditional Thanksgiving dinner with both sets of parents, we celebrated by turning on our exterior lights for the holiday season as we had hoped. The next day, Steve and I set out to enjoy another tradition we were building into our family life. Steve and his family had always had a real tree when he was growing up, and it was important to him to keep that tradition. So, having both taken Friday off from our jobs, we were set to relish our shared experience again this year. Driving to a tree farm, seeking the perfect Douglas fir, wrestling it onto the car and getting it home for decoration was usually fun for both of us. Even though I had always had an artificial tree due to allergies until my teenage years, I loved our tree selection day. Because Steve and I always wanted Christmas to be a special time for our family, selecting a tree and decorating it together was a big part of our holiday.

Sadly, though, instead of enjoying our outing as I usually did, I was just on automatic, wandering around the tree farm, barely aware of the blustery wind and unseasonably mild temperature. I couldn't generate any excitement because I felt oozy and exhausted. I truly did not even care if I was there or not. Typically, Steve and I would wander from row to row looking for that perfect tree that would fill the special place set aside for it and display our growing collection of treasured ornaments. This year, I just wanted to get back home to rest, so I was agreeable to any tree Steve saw that he liked. I stood observing all the families making memories, and I did find joy in hearing little ones yell in excitement that this one or that one over there was the perfect tree. I watched with anticipation of the time next year, when we, too, would have a little one in tow. I pictured us going from row to row looking for our very own perfect tree, taking photos on our smartphones, and creating our precious family memories. But, at that moment, the more we roamed the farm, the worse I felt.
Disappointed that something I so enjoyed had become such a chore, I kept wishing I would turn the feel-better corner everyone promised was just ahead. But for me in this pregnancy, the corner never seemed to come.

December 2002

Our house, like others in our neighborhood, looked festive with its blaze of colored lights, and our tree was lovingly and artistically decorated. As we drew nearer to the holiday, I remained hopeful that I would have the energy to bake cookies, an activity that was a cherished tradition for me. I remembered, as a girl, nagging my mom to make Christmas cookies even though it was only the first week in December. My mom was an excellent cook and baker, and she was always busy creating magic in our kitchen. I knew my love for baking was set in stone because each time my mom was done mixing a sweet treat, she would allow me to lick the beaters from the mixer before washing them. Thinking of long-ago Christmases, I remembered one of my most treasured gifts was an Easy-Bake Oven from Santa. Oh how I would be so excited to mix and make my little cakes and watch closely as they were cooked by what looked to be a light bulb.

Now, standing in the kitchen of my suburban home, I was fighting back nausea, trying to keep the Christmas cookie tradition going. Most cookies coming from the oven on December 20 were destined for Steve's Christmas party in Rochester. He had been commuting back and forth between offices for months now. I was determined to make a large cookie platter for his colleagues to enjoy. Every other part of my life had lost its balance and this was one tradition I wanted desperately to keep. I hadn't done a thing for a few days as I was not well enough to work consecutive days. I felt emotionally stale. I needed to accomplish something. Creating beautifully decorated, delicious cookies for others to enjoy seemed as if it would be a cure for my malaise.

"I'm going to do this," I said to our beloved beagle, Maude, as she basked in the sun on the floral couch. Maude perked up at the sound of my voice and looked my way.

"You can be my taste tester," I promised. Maybe if I spoke positively of the things I so wanted to do, they would actually come about. As I prepared cookie batter, I thought about all my female friends who had been encouraging me for months already to keep my spirits up and look forward to the time when my health would improve. That was supposed to happen after the first trimester.

"You'll turn the corner," they kept assuring me as they sensed my discouragement. "You will."

As well-meaning friends shared their own stories of morning sickness and sleepiness, I accepted their concern, but–without being dramatic–I knew that I was strong enough to endure the normal discomforts of the first trimester. That special insight I'd had since childhood told me that what I was experiencing was something beyond the usual symptoms friends described.

In my reverie, I admitted to myself that I had grown frustrated hearing I would turn a corner and I was even more frustrated that it had not happened. My mom, so concerned for my well-being, called daily asking the same thing. "Are you feeling any better today?" she'd ask, the sense of hope evident in her question. I'd try to be positive, telling her that I did think I was feeling better. But she was my mother after all, so she could always discern the truth. We had the same conversation for months.

As it turns out, the conclusion of my first trimester in October did bring me mental, if not physical, relief. The chance of a second miscarriage had been reduced significantly. The twelve-week mark was my milestone, and I had nurtured myself to make it to that point. It had been back in early February of 2002 that Steve and I learned my first pregnancy would end in miscarriage at seven weeks. No wonder, then, that we felt apprehensive about this one.

Now we were almost into a new year, and as I scraped the cookie dough off the beaters with my spatula, I felt my stomach jump as if the baby was jumping rope. The movement was much stronger than anything I'd felt up to that point and it struck me as being unusual. I immediately put my right hand on my stomach and felt the baby thrashing around. The movement was extensive, but I did not feel any pain.

Then, after a minute or two, the movement stopped. I felt nothing. I put my right hand back on my stomach and stood very still, waiting to feel the movement again. Nothing. With my heart beating fast, I left everything on the counter and walked to the sunroom to lie on the couch. In the quiet, I turned from side to side trying to entice movement from my baby. A kick, a roll, anything from my baby. After several minutes, I headed into the kitchen and went right to the closet. The doctor always told me if I ever felt worried about the lack of movement to have candy or juice to help the baby become a little more active. I grabbed a Snickers bar, tore off the wrapper and forced myself to gobble it, washing it down with apple juice. I registered that the cookie batter was still sitting in the mixer. The flour, sugar, and measuring cups were a mess on the counter. As soon as I felt the baby move, I would get back to it, and I'd continue the process of baking and decorating holiday treats.

"God, let everything be okay," I said out loud. Faithful Maude, sleeping next to me on the couch, perked her head up. She had been my support lately, cuddling with me on the days when I could barely do a thing.

"I'm scared," I told her. "Terrified" would have been a more precise choice of words. My special sense of signs and circumstances came into play. Deep in my heart, I knew something dreadful had taken place in those few minutes in my beautifully decorated home as I was trying to go about my usual holiday activities. I could no longer bear this knowledge alone.

I picked up the phone and called Steve. "I don't feel the baby moving," I said, as soon as he answered. Steve knew the routine the doctor had suggested as well as I did.

"Did you eat a candy bar or drink some juice?"

"Yes! And Steve...I don't feel the baby moving." It's all I could think of, and he heard the panic in my voice.

"Call the doctor's office," he said. From his work, an hour away, Steve offered the best solution he could, and it was the right one.

I could barely wait for the receptionist to answer. When she did, I blurted it all out in one breath.

"Hi. My name is Jenny Haust and I am a patient of Dr. Randolph's. I am six months pregnant and have not felt my baby moving for a while. I have eaten a candy bar and drunk a glass of juice and still am not feeling any movement. I am really worried." I gasped for breath.

"Can you come right in?" the receptionist asked.

"I will be right there," I whispered.

I grabbed my pink fleece jacket off the coat hanger, pulled it on and quickly got into the car for the twenty-five minute drive. It was bitter cold, but I could feel the warmth of the winter sun on my face as I passed the NYS Fairgrounds on Route 690. Despite the cold, we had not had our first snow yet, so roads were clear and, at that time of day, free of heavy traffic. I talked to myself out loud all the way there. “Everything is fine, don’t worry. Please God, let everything be all right. The baby has to be fine.”

I have no memory of finding a parking spot, turning off the engine, and walking into the medical building. Somehow, I was entering the office.

Lori, Dr. Randolph's nurse, saw me immediately and set me up for a sonogram. She put the Doppler on my belly. It was familiar and cold. I kept wiping my sweaty hands on my pants, which were still dusted with flour. I was waiting to recognize that beautiful rapid heartbeat I had been hearing for months. But there was nothing. Complete silence. Lori moved the Doppler all around my belly as I lay on the table and kept a close watch on her facial expression. I could see that she seemed concerned. But she smiled as she set the equipment down.

“I’m going to go get Claire, the nurse practitioner,” she said. “Claire will help locate the heartbeat. I will be right back.”

I sat in silence. All I could hear was the buzz of the fluorescent light and the crunching sound of the paper on the examining table as I moved. I was still unsure of what to think, hoping for good news, yet dreading the worst.

Lori came back with Claire, and after several attempts to locate a heartbeat, Claire whispered, "I can't find the baby's heartbeat." She took the sonogram device and put it on my belly and turned the monitor on. I turned my head so I could look at the computer screen, and I lifted my head to see my baby on the monitor. My baby looked great. I could see a perfectly formed tiny head, body, hands, and little feet. But everything I feared deep down seemed all too accurate. The baby was very still. There was no heartbeat. I couldn't speak. My body was frozen, but my heart was racing.

"Do you want me to call Steve?" Lori asked. At that moment, I knew that everything I dreaded was coming true. I wanted to go back in time, back to the kitchen before everything went wrong. I wondered if even something as simple as baking cookies was more than I should have attempted. How could I fix things, I wondered? I realized Lori had asked me a question and I hadn't responded.

I could barely speak or even look at her. "I will call him," I replied.

Lori took me by my arm and helped me off the exam table. She helped me into Dr. Randolph's quiet office, walked around to his side of the desk and picked up the phone to bring it to me as I sank into a chair. In slow motion, I picked up the phone and dialed Steve's cell number. It was painful to touch the numbers.

"Hello? Hello? Daint?" he said, using his special name for me.

"I'm at the doctor's office and they can't find the heartbeat," I blurted out. "Come right away."

"I'm on my way," he said.

I handed the phone to Lori, sat in the chair, and stared at the wall. Waiting for my husband, I tried to understand what was happening, but I couldn't grasp it. Everything, all our hopes and plans for a child, had shifted in the span of a few minutes. I felt as if I should be doing something, but all I could do was wait.

Steve arrived from Rochester about an hour later. He spoke with Lori and Claire about what we needed to do. Lori gave us instructions and directions to a radiology office in Fayetteville, a 15-mile drive. She told Steve that after we went to the Fayetteville office, we would need to go to St. Joseph's Hospital as soon as possible. Steve helped me out of the chair and supported me as we walked out of Dr. Randolph's office.

I kept my head down and did not make eye contact with anyone in the waiting room. Steve helped me into the passenger side of the car and shut the door. As I watched him walk around to the driver's side, I automatically reached for my seatbelt and pulled it around my belly. I felt like a robot, completely outside of myself. We drove in silence to Fayetteville, neither of us daring to express either hope or despair. I simply could not speak. I just stared out the passenger side window, not even registering what I was looking at. Suddenly, I was jolted into consciousness by a familiar sight.

As we drove up Route 5, we passed a small pond where geese had gathered. The water shimmered in the light of the bright winter sun, and the feathers of all the geese shone like beautiful silk. There they were again–geese, those migrating birds that signaled the changing seasons.

We arrived in the eastern suburb of Fayetteville ten minutes later. I tried not to make eye contact with anyone when we entered the office. It was a small place with only a few chairs. The receptionist told me to sit down, and they would be right with us. I knew I was a mess, clothing in disarray, still flecked with flour and sugar, and my hair messy from having lain on the examination table at the other office. My eyes were burning, red and swollen. An older woman sat with her teenage daughter in the cramped waiting area. I tried not to cry because I didn't want to alarm them, but I did. I wept. I just kept my head down and kept wiping my eyes and nose with my wadded-up, soaked tissue.
Fortunately, we weren't made to wait. I was called into a dark room right away, and the radiologist took a detailed look with the sonogram as a small

group of residents observed in absolute silence. The silence was broken when the radiologist confirmed my worst fears. My baby had died. It was the first time someone had said it. Dead.

I couldn't get off the table. I felt paralyzed. Steve gently reached for one arm and lifted me. I told him I needed to use the restroom. We headed into the hall of the main building, and I opened the door to the restroom to find it was just one big room with a toilet. I stumbled inside and quickly closed and locked the door behind me. "Dead." I fell to my knees, then I just lay on the filthy floor and cried.

I don't know how long I lay there, but eventually I forced myself to use the toilet, wash my hands, and splash cold water on my reddened face. I slowly opened the door and found the woman and her teenage daughter from the radiology office standing there. How long they had been waiting, I'll never know.

"Can we do anything for you?" the woman asked. I recognized the look of pity in her eyes, but I couldn't speak to thank her for her concern. Instead, I only shook my head no.

"We are so very sorry," the mother said. It was a phrase I would hear repeated hundreds of times in the weeks to come, and it always let me know that people cared.

Back on 690, driving home to pick up clothing, I felt something I'd been holding inside me give way. As I looked out the window toward Onondaga Lake, my silence turned to hysteria. I felt like jumping out of the car. I banged my hands on the dashboard. I screamed and wailed.

"Please calm down," Steve begged. His emotions must have been in turmoil, too, after receiving my panicked phone call, driving from Rochester to Syracuse with so much uncertainty, and then learning the terrible news. But somehow, he got us home safely.

"Call my mom, please, just call my mom," I said to Steve when we reached the driveway.

As I opened the door, Maude Lilly jumped with excitement at seeing me. But even her innocent greeting could not help me. I walked straight upstairs to my closet and filled a bag with necessary items: a toothbrush, my glasses, contact lens solution, and hairbrush. The hospital was our next destination, and we had been told to get there as soon as we could. There was no time to put away the baking supplies or tidy the kitchen. Within minutes we were back in the car, Steve driving back into the city again.

We arrived at St. Joseph's and took the elevator up to the labor and delivery floor.

"I need your license for identification," the nurse at the admitting desk said.

I handed her my license, but I couldn't make eye contact.

Adhering to routine, she put an identification band on my wrist and showed me to a private room. It was like a cave. The room was painted clay orange, and there were no windows streaming natural light to soften the institutional fluorescence. The only pieces of furniture were a bed and a rocking chair.

I was assigned to the physician on call, a further source of anguish because I felt uneasy not having Dr. Randolph, who had been with me every step of the way from my first miscarriage to seeing me regularly through this pregnancy. I knew he deserved time to relax with his family, but at that moment, I desperately wanted him to come back from vacation. I changed into a hospital gown and threw my pink fleece jacket over me for a bit of comfort and warmth. Soon, a doctor came into my cave and introduced himself as Dr. Mark Wright.

"I will be taking care of you until I am done with my shift. I am very sorry for your loss," he said, looking over my chart. "Typically, under these circumstances, we will go ahead and induce. Just as we would in a normal pregnancy. You will deliver your baby vaginally."

"Why?" I asked, frightened and horrified. "Why must I deliver this baby while I am awake? Can't you put me under and deliver my baby via C-section?" I knew I sounded desperate.

Dr. Wright assured me this was the healthiest way for my body not only now but going forward. He explained to me the steps that would take place. He left briefly to instruct the staff to start the typical birthing induction drugs. He had told me I would have my baby at some point over the next twenty-four hours.

Dr. Wright returned to the cave to speak with Steve and me. He told us we had to make some decisions about how we wanted to deal with the baby after delivery.

"I need to know if you are going to want an autopsy," he said.

I looked at Steve and he looked at me. We didn't speak. We didn't even know what to say.

"I'll give you some time to discuss this," Dr. Wright said.

After a brief discussion, Steve and I decided that we did want an autopsy. Perhaps we would then have an explanation for the death of our baby. We signed the consent form. One more deeply wounding procedural bit of red tape.

I shivered from the drugs and the stark, chilly cave. I held tightly onto my pink fleece jacket. It was the one thing around me that was not hospital oriented. I hated the gown, the drugs, the sterile environment, and most of all, the hospital smell.

My mom and dad arrived late in the afternoon. They cried when they saw me. I put my hand over my mouth and could not speak. I wondered how I would ever feel normal again. I was waiting for my baby to come into this world, and we knew the baby would not make that first cry that parents anticipate. The thought of knowing I was carrying a dead baby inside of my body made me feel sick. Knowing I had to deliver the baby naturally made me feel even worse. I felt disgusting.

"This is a very difficult situation," Dr. Wright explained to Steve and me. "Losing a baby takes a heavy toll on not only you as an individual, but also as a couple." He was forthright in his discussions with us. We understood his concern and his intent to be helpful, but we could barely wrap our minds around the horror of the past twenty-four hours, let alone look ahead. Everyone on staff tried to engage us in conversation and help us move forward.

"Do you know what the sex of the baby is?" Mary, my nurse, asked.

"No. We were waiting until the baby was born," I replied, thinking of our decision to simply love this baby whether it was a boy or a girl.

Steve's parents arrived at the hospital late afternoon. Steve spoke with them, explaining all that had transpired. He asked if they could go to our home and feed Maude. That was a relief to me, as I didn't want anyone around me. I didn't want to make conversation; I didn't want to explain what had happened leading up to this moment.

Steve and I had many decisions ahead of us. We talked about what we should name our baby. Although we had given some thought to names, we hadn't yet come to a final decision. Now, for this child, we decided that if it was a boy, we would name him Steve and if the baby was a girl, we would name her Jenny. It made sense to us.

Mary came back and sat next to me. "I need to ask you another question," she said.

I looked at her inquisitively. With true compassion, Mary asked, "Would you like to hold your baby when he or she is born?"

"No," I said immediately. Initially, I was appalled at the thought of holding my dead child. All the months of pregnancy, this is one matter that never occurred to me.

Mary looked surprised. I explained that I felt by holding my baby, it would make letting go even more difficult. I told Steve he should make the decision for himself.

"Jenny, you should really think about holding your baby," Mary said. I sensed she wanted me to think about it a bit.

"Under the circumstances, it might be wise to hold your baby in order to be able to feel some closure."

I thought about it as I lay there. I started to think about my baby actually being born. This would be my first experience giving birth. What would I do? Would they just take the baby away if I chose not to hold him or her? Would I never get to see my baby? The more I thought about it, the more I understood that Mary was right. I needed to hold this child as much as he or she needed to be held.

I grew tired and dozed off and on. Dr. Wright came to tell me his shift had ended, but I could call him if I needed to. He said his partner, Dr. Connor, would be on duty and that I would be in good hands. I could see the compassion for me in Dr. Wright's eyes.

I clung to my pink fleece jacket for warmth. I fell in and out of sleep, waking to see my mom sitting in the rocking chair under the dim light, while Steve slept on a cot in the corner.

"You are going to get through this," my mom whispered. "Please try and rest," she said.

I closed my eyes only to open them every so often to see my mom rocking in the chair under the small light keeping watch over me.

I woke up soaking wet.

"Your water broke," the nurse said.

My mom jumped up and tended to me along with the nurses. It was 2 a.m.

"Steve, wake up!" my mom yelled. He did not wake. She went over and shook him.

"I feel like I need to push," I said. I began to panic.

The nurses hurried in and quickly set up the delivery equipment.

"Where is the doctor?" I yelled.

The room was dark. The only light shone from a large lamp the staff had wheeled in to assist the doctor in delivery. Everyone was half asleep.

At 2:34 a.m. my baby girl, Jenny Rebecca, was born. She weighed 1.4 pounds.

The nurse wrapped her tightly in a little blanket and handed her to me. All I could see was her tiny face. She was beautiful. She was covered in little blond fuzz and looked like a beautiful tiny angel. I wept as I stared at her. I couldn't understand why this precious little girl was not granted the gift of life, why she would never coo in her crib, go to ballet classes, join me in making Christmas cookies, and grow to have a family of her own.

I handed her to Steve. He held her gingerly, and she looked so tiny in his arms.

"Mom, do you want to hold her?" I asked. She cried as she took this beautiful, fragile baby from Steve.

My mom held her for several minutes before giving her back to me.

"Please hold her for as long as you need," the nurse said.

And so I did. I studied her. I carefully unfolded the blanket from around her tiny hands. She was absolutely perfect looking. I found it hard to believe she was dead.

I kept staring and studying her so that I would remember her face for the rest of my life. I didn't ever want to forget what she looked like or any small detail of this perfect, tiny baby. At length, having imprinted every sweet aspect of my first child on my memory and with one last kiss, I handed her to the nurse.

Despite my anguish, and perhaps with the help of medication, I did sleep. The next morning, I felt like I was in a black hole.

"How are you doing, Jenny?" the nurse asked.

I wanted to scream, "How do you think I am doing?" But, of course, I gave the expected response, which I would use so often in the weeks ahead: "I'm doing fine, thank you."

She asked if I wanted to be moved to the post-delivery area. I could hear a woman in labor screaming from down the hall. This added to my fury.

"No! I want to go home as soon as possible," I told the nurse.

My brother had taken the first flight he could from Florida and brought me a little white ceramic snowman filled with flowers, Christmas greens, and green glass Christmas bulbs. It looked tiny in his hands, just as Jenny had looked in my arms. I could see the sadness he felt for me.

"Would you like any medication to help calm you?" the nurse asked.

"I don't need any drugs," I responded.

The nurse informed me I would be discharged by lunchtime as long as I was feeling well.

"I just want to go home," I said. But, of course, going home is not a simple procedure.

The nurse arrived with a bunch of paperwork.

"I need to review all this with you prior to discharge," she said.

I saw her mouth moving as she spoke and pointed at the paperwork. I probably nodded my head as if I understood, but I really didn't hear her. But, when the discharge paperwork had been completed, I was free to go, and the nurse instructed Steve to bring the car around.

As I sat in a wheelchair waiting to be taken to meet Steve at the main entrance, a volunteer arrived at the room, an African American woman. She helped me into the wheelchair and took me to the patient elevator. We did not speak. When the doors opened to the lobby decorated for Christmas, I realized the holiday that I loved was now forever changed. Still, we did not speak.

The automatic door to the entrance of the hospital opened and a rush of cold air hit me. Again, as I had so many times throughout this ordeal, I wrapped my fleece jacket tightly around me. Cold, weary, and overwhelmed, I felt empty leaving the hospital without my baby. The woman, who had silently wheeled me to this point, looked at me, touched my arm and whispered, "God bless you."

Hearing those words, I was overcome with a deep sense of calm. Something in her presence, her kindness, her blessing, had begun to heal me. I was certain then, as I watched her wheel the chair away, that I would return to St. Joseph's Hospital. Next time, I would leave with a baby in my arms.

I was enveloped in an aura of wonder as Steve helped me out of the wheelchair and into the car. The door slammed shut from the wind. We drove along Onondaga Lake Parkway in silence. It was a clear, cold winter day. A few snow flurries fell, the first of the season. I felt exhausted.

"Do you need anything? Do you want me to stop anywhere?" Steve asked. "Are you hungry?"

"No. I just want to go home," I replied.

Coming Home

Steve raised the garage door and drove inside. I opened the door to the laundry area from the garage, and I was instantly greeted by Maude Lilly. She barked, wagged her tail, and whined with joy at my presence.

"Hi pretty girl," I said as I bent over to pet her. I was home at last and Maude Lilly provided a slight sense of normalcy.

"I'm so happy to see you, too," I said. My dear little beagle knew nothing of the hell I had been through as I continued to pet her. It felt refreshing to have such joyful energy directed toward me. From the moment in Dr. Randolph 's office when the nurse knew something was wrong, to the look of shock and pity on the residents' faces while they observed the confirmation of my child's death, to the delivery, I had been overwhelmed by the sorrow of so many. The way everyone in the hospital had looked upon me with pity had been devastating. Maude's joy was welcome and the presence of my family was comforting.

"How are you doing?" my dad asked.

"I'm tired and just need to rest," I told him.

"Mom and I are here for whatever you need."

"Thanks, dad. I know you are."

My brother was standing in the sun room. I don't think he really knew what to say. I knew he felt horrible for me. So, in reality, he didn't really need to say anything at all.

"I'm going to go take a shower, put some pajamas on and lie in bed," I announced to everyone.

I felt awkward in my own home for some reason. I didn't feel normal.

The warm water felt good on my body. I didn't move from under the shower head. I just stood there. I wanted to wash away any hint of being at St. Joseph's Hospital. I held my hands up to my face and kept splashing handfuls of water over my eyes. I started to cry.

"I need some strength," I whispered. "Please give me some strength."

As I used the towel to dry myself off, I noticed it was becoming stained. I looked down and noticed blood running down my legs.

"Jesus," I said, as I ran to grab toilet paper and a large pad from a bag of pads and bed liners they had given to me at the hospital. I got myself situated and cozy in my pajamas. I felt some comfort from the shower and wearing fresh pajamas that were my own.

"Hi sweet girl," I said to Maude as she sat on my bed staring at me.

"Oh girl, you're so sweet," I said, as I felt her velvet ears.

I threw the decorative pillows off the bed one by one, tugged at my fluffy comforter, and made a spot for myself to settle in. I laid a large plastic liner from the hospital down on my side so I didn't bleed through onto my bed sheets if I happened to fall asleep. I pulled the covers up close and took my glasses off. I stared at the large Christmas tree covered in white lights in our room. The lights looked blurry, but so pretty and peaceful to me. My mind racing and my body tired, I tried to relax. I kept thinking how I wanted to crawl into a hole and make this all go away. I didn't want to deal with this. I could feel Maude's warmth next to me. I fell asleep.

I awoke and looked at the clock. I had been asleep for two hours. I felt groggy and lay there staring at the Christmas tree while Maude was still snuggled in next to me.

I made my way slowly to the bathroom. I was still bleeding from having given birth. I wondered where it could all possibly be coming from. I stared at myself in the mirror and found it hard to believe what I had been through. This couldn't have possibly happened to me, I thought in my mind. I turned the water on and splashed my face several times. I looked in the mirror again to confirm this was actually my reality. It was. I wanted to get in bed and never get out. After drying my face, I took a deep breath and headed back downstairs with Maude following right behind me.

"Are you going to be all right?" My brother asked as he stood in the kitchen. "Are you going to go off the deep end?"

I paused, letting his words echo into the silence.

What a strange question to ask, I thought.

Maybe it was something everyone was concerned about, but I knew my own strength and, although I was suffering, I would not do anything to cause harm.

"I don't think so," I finally replied.

"That hadn't crossed my mind," I assured him.

The doctor and staff at the hospital had asked me about taking something to help with my emotions and I told them I didn't want to take anything. I didn't want to dull my feelings. I didn't want this to come back at me years down the road. I needed to try to deal with it head on. I did feel devastated, but I didn't feel broken. For some reason, the day I left the hospital seemed to stick with me. I kept thinking about the lady who wheeled me to the car. There was something about her, about her hand on me. Her touch calmed me. I knew right then I would come back there someday and leave with a baby.

"That lady at the hospital." I paused for a moment, knowing how hard it would be to communicate that miraculous encounter that had taken place so quickly and that was so deeply personal to me. "When she touched my arm. Brent, there was something about her." I looked at my brother. "It's something that I can't explain or even understand myself."

My brother stared at me as if he couldn't grasp what I was saying. I began to think he was worried for me. I know he was wondering how I was going to recover from this. I was feeling terrible, but I felt I needed to reassure him.

"I will be okay," I said. "Don't worry about me."

Brent still looked worried, but he accepted my response and didn't push the topic any further.

The phone was ringing. It was my best friend, Lisa.

"Are you okay, Jen?" she asked as her voice cracked.

I had a hard time responding to her. My best friend, Lis. She lived in the house behind me growing up. We were inseparable as young girls. We swam in my pool almost every day in the summer, slept over at each other's house more times than not. We loved watching MTV while devouring our own large containers of Planters Cheez Balls after a fun day of bike riding around the neighborhood and roller skating in her driveway. She was the sister I never had. Both of us complete opposites, hence, why we got along so well. And we both loved Christmas. Always decorating our bedroom windows with lights and lighting a small tree in our rooms to celebrate the season. I always knew when she was home and awake at the holidays by the lights in her window and she knew the same about me.

"I'm okay, Lis. I am," I told her as I started to cry.

"I'm here for you, for whatever you may need," she replied.

I knew Lis would always support me. She had demonstrated that since we were little girls. And, although I faced sadness greater than any I had experienced before, I knew I was not alone in my grief. I had so many people who were concerned for our family, so many who cared about me. And Lis was one of them.

I thanked her and hung up.

I sat on the couch and heard the doorbell ring. Maude started barking. My dad grabbed her while my brother answered the door. He carried a bouquet of pure white roses.

My dad took them from Brent and placed them on the table in front of me.

I pulled the small card from its holder. Written in script was a comforting message from our friends Mike and Jackie. I held the roses to my nose. One of my favorite flowers. The aroma instantly took me back, as it always did, to when I was seven and my Pop Pop passed away. I remember my dad picking me up so I could see Pop Pop in his casket at the funeral home. I wanted to say goodbye. I remember grabbing a beautiful single red flower that was lying next to him in the casket and keeping it. I did not know then it was a rose. But I never forgot that aroma.

"Are you okay with Brent, dad and I heading back home in a few hours? We think it's important for you and Steve to have some privacy," my mom said.

"Go ahead, mom. It's okay," I said as I hugged her.

Christmas was just three days away.

"Why don't you both drive down with the dog when you are ready," my dad said.

I watched as my parents and brother pulled out of the driveway. I felt as if I was watching a movie and that this was not my real life. This terrible thing couldn't possibly happen to me.

It seemed awfully quiet for the first time in days.

Steve and I were alone, and we were both exhausted. I told him I needed to rest, and I fell into a deep sleep only to be woken hours later in agony. My breasts were throbbing.

I sat up straight in bed.

"What's wrong?" Steve asked.

"My boobs are killing me. They are throbbing," I told him.

"I have no idea why. Maybe if I take a shower that will help."

The warm water did not provide any relief. It actually made them throb even more. They were swollen. Painful to the touch, and when I started to dry myself off, the pressure of the towel made me wince.

"You need to call the doctor's office as soon as they get in," Steve said. I followed his advice and reached the receptionist just minutes after the practice opened. I told her what was happening and described my pain.

"You may be engorged," a kind voice on the other end of the phone said.

"What's engorged?" I asked.

"When you give birth, your breasts will start to make milk in the first couple of days. If you don't breastfeed, this can happen. They can become swollen and painful. It should get better after several days," the nurse explained reassuringly.

"Put a tight sports bra on right away, if you have one, and wear it even while you sleep. Make sure it's really tight. You can also take some ibuprofen and apply cold compresses if needed. Call us back right away if you develop a fever. Okay?"

"Okay," I replied and hung up.

"What did she say?" Steve asked.

"She thinks I am engorged," I replied.

He looked at me confused. I went on to tell him what that meant.

I walked over to the kitchen counter and grabbed the folder from the hospital. It was a record of my stay there along with post-discharge instructions. It was at that moment that I realized the nurse had reviewed all of this prior to me leaving. I must have been in shock or something when the nurse was speaking to me and I didn't actually hear anything she was saying. I felt foolish for allowing this to happen. Had I listened to her instructions, I could have prevented this. I was pissed at myself.

I went upstairs and grabbed a black sports bra out of my closet.

"Ouch, Ouch, Ouch," I said aloud, as I squeezed it over my head and onto the rest of my upper body.

"Can you get me some ibuprofen?" I yelled down to Steve.

“Here, I brought the entire container up in case you need more,” Steve said as he handed me a glass of water.

“I need to lie down for a while,” I told him.

I climbed back into bed. Maude jumped in with me. As I lay my head on the pillow, I stared at the Christmas tree. The white lights now clear as I still had my glasses on. It wasn't nearly as pretty as when the lights were blurry. I took my glasses off, glanced over at the blurry lights on the tree, and snuggled in with Maude.

“What am I going to do?” I whispered.

I thought Maude would open her eyes when she heard my voice, but she didn’t. She was completely happily snuggled in with me. I could hear by her deep breathing that she had fallen into a deep sleep already. Perfectly content. I listened to her breathing and eventually fell asleep, too.

I woke up several hours later. I couldn't tell if Steve was home or not. I walked downstairs. He was working on his laptop catching up on emails.

“Have you heard from the funeral home?” I asked Steve.

“No,” he replied.

“We need to figure out what comes next,” I said.

I hadn't given much thought to what came next. I felt overwhelmed by the past several days. Since we decided to have an autopsy done on baby Jenny, I didn't know what would come next. No one told us. I wasn't sure if we had a formal funeral or exactly how something like this was handled. Knowing it was the Christmas holiday caused even more confusion.

"Steve and I are trying to figure out what the next few days will bring," I said to my mom on the other end of the phone.

"Did you speak to the funeral home?" she asked.

"No. I will have Steve call and ask about burial plans."

Later, I asked Steve, "What did the funeral home say?"

"They are waiting on us for burial details. We need to figure out where we will bury the baby and let them know."

Steve's mom had reached out to the cemetery in Johnson City to check details about having a burial there. Her family had a plot there already so she was familiar with the place.

"Do you know where the cemetery is?" Steve asked.

"Yes. My friend Dan's father was buried there back in high school after passing from cancer. I remember exactly where it is."

Steve had spoken with his mom and we needed to go there and inquire about the burial for baby Jenny.

Do they have burials in December? I wondered.

I picked up the phone and dialed the number I had written in pencil.

A man answered the other end of the phone.

"Are you open on Christmas Eve?" I asked.

He said he would be there and asked how he could help.

I explained to him what had happened and that our infant daughter was at a local funeral home.

"I am calling to check to see if we could stop by on Christmas Eve to inquire about a potential cemetery plot and what our options might be. We should be there around 10. Would that be okay?" I asked.

He assured me he would be there.

We packed up and headed to Endwell to my parents' house early on Christmas Eve. We dropped Maude Lilly off at their house and headed to the cemetery where we pulled into the front main entrance. It was all coming back to me as I remembered being here back in the 12th grade on a beautiful sunny day to honor Dan's dad's passing. Today, it was overcast and wintry. The sky was full of several shades of gray. Not a stitch of sunshine around.

Just past the entrance a single small brown brick building stood on the left with a small parking lot to the right of it. We pulled in, parked, and headed through the front door.

A nice man named Dennis greeted us each with a handshake.

"I am Jenny and this is my husband, Steve. I spoke to you the other day on the phone."

"Yes," he replied. "I'm very sorry for your loss."

"Thank you," I said, my voice cracking.

He had a large paper photo display grid of the cemetery and the current plots available along with planned phases. I noticed this was a Catholic cemetery. I wasn't sure this would be an appropriate place for us.

"Can I ask you a question?" I said softly to Dennis.

"I'm not Catholic, so I am unsure if this is going to work for us to buy a plot here. Steve is, but I am not. Jenny would have been baptized in the Episcopal Church. So, I need clarification on this before we go any further."

"It is no problem, Jenny. You are perfectly okay to buy a plot here and have your infant daughter buried here," Dennis kindly replied.

He invited us to sit.

"We don't know anything about this process," I explained.

I guess in reality most people don't. Why would anyone have good reason to unless they had suffered the loss of a loved one? These situations are forced on you. They are never choices. Well, unless you're one of those people that plans for everything, including death. All these things went through my mind as I sat watching Dennis take a folder out from his desk. He placed it on the desk and turned it toward us so that he could review everything with Steve and me.

"So, you have a few choices in this particular situation," Dennis explained.

"We have a nice area of the cemetery where people who have lost children or infants like yourself can choose to bury your loved one. Our other option is for you and Steve to purchase a plot where you will be buried someday. What we would do is bury your infant daughter deeper than typical and your casket would be placed on top of her someday. It would be up to you on which side you would like that to happen. Jenny, you can be buried above her, or Steve, you could be buried above her."

I swallowed.

"Are you okay?" Steve asked.

I cleared my throat and sniffed so I didn't need a tissue.

I was having difficulty. All this talk of death. Me at 30 years old and Steve at 35 trying to figure out where our final resting place will be.

"Maybe we should bury her in the special section," Steve said.

I looked at him in confusion. I wasn't sure what the best option would be. The more I thought about it, the more uncomfortable I felt. Having her off on her own seemed so lonely and isolating. I liked the second option Dennis presented to us. Knowing that someday I would be buried with my infant daughter brought me some peace. I would finally be with her after living my physical life without her. It would be almost like a full circle moment to me as I reasoned this decision in my mind.

"We should buy our plot, Steve," I said aloud.

Dennis referred back to the large cemetery map he had displayed on an easel next to his desk. He pointed out that in the upper corner of the cemetery was a newly opened section.

"Why don't we get in the car and go take a look at this area?" Dennis suggested.

We drove on the outer perimeter of the cemetery and headed up a slight hill. Almost to the top, Dennis stopped and exited his car.

Steve and I followed.

To the left side of our cars, Dennis walked along a grassy area that was full of markers. The section was flat and butted up to a really nice, wooded area. The trees were bare, and I could see deep into the woods. I was taken at the beauty of the depth of the woods and the peace I felt looking through the trees.

This area is where we would be able to purchase a plot.

It all looked the same. We noticed a few trees that must have been planted in the spring.

"This looks good. Right here beneath this newly planted tree," I said.

"They all look the same to me," Steve replied.

Being buried under a nice tree gave me some comfort. I have no idea why. Nothing seemed to make sense to me. Perhaps I was looking for a moment to breathe and Mother Nature was my catalyst.

We drove back down the drive and went into Dennis's office. He began filling out paperwork. It was so quiet.

On the morning of Christmas Eve, Steve and I wrote a check for $935.00 as a down payment on Section 35 burial plot 167.

"You'll have a balance of $835.00 that will need to be paid in 11 monthly installments of $69.60 each. Your final installment of $69.40 will then pay your plot in full. Will that work for you?" Dennis asked.

I would be making monthly payments on a burial plot just as I had on my old Honda Prelude until it was paid in full. Coupon book and all. How awful, I thought.

Dennis explained that after the plot was paid in full, we could then have a headstone placed. He would give us a list of suppliers that the cemetery did business with and that they were well aware of the requirements for the design of the headstone.

"Can you please review what the requirements are?" I asked.

"The stone must have some sort of religious symbol on it. Our suppliers are aware of our requirements. They will do a mockup for you and then send it to us for approval. There are some rules and regulations about what needs to be on the headstone. The diocese will then have to approve what you will have out on the headstone prior to ordering it. Upon approval, they will then send it to production. Here is a list of local monument suppliers. If you have any questions, please do not hesitate to reach out to me."

Dennis handed us our folder with all our information, and we shook his hand and left. It was just about noon.

"Do you think we should go right away to a few of these places on the list?" I asked.

Steve was as confused as I was. We expected to be caring for our baby, not burying her.

"Let's try to find this place on the list that is close and see if they are open," I said.

A few minutes later we pulled up to a small, single-story building located on a corner. It was a little white brick building on a residential street. It had a white metal awning over the large front window. It reminded me of the brown metal awning my grandmother's house had when I was a little girl. I noticed it was located directly across from a funeral home. How fitting, I thought. I don't think I would have ever noticed this place had we not been looking for it. We had to park on the street in front of the building. There were no other cars around. I assumed they were closed. There was no sign to indicate either way. We pushed on the door, and it opened.

"May I help you?" an older woman asked.

I explained we had just purchased a plot and would need to order a headstone.

"Can you help us?" I asked.

We sat down at a small desk just as we had at the cemetery.

"Is this for you?" she asked.

"Yes," we said as we explained to her what had happened.

She pulled out a piece of paper from her drawer and proceeded to go through pricing. She never even told us her name or asked ours.

"We have some monuments here in the store to look at," she said, pointing to the corner, robotic in her gestures.

"What are you looking to have on the stone?"

"Well, we're not sure. We were given a sheet from the cemetery that shows the headstone requirements," Steve said.

I began to feel uncomfortable.

"I'm ready to go," I insisted to Steve.

"Really?" he replied.

"Yes. Let's go."

I stood up from my chair and just looked at the woman. I felt angry toward her for some reason. I put the pricing sheet she had given us back on her desk and stared at her for a moment. I didn't say anything as I picked up my purse off the floor and walked out.

"What happened?" Steve asked as he got in the car.

"That lady. She was so rude. I'm not buying anything here," I said with disgust.

"Okay," he said as he started the car.

"Let's look over the sheet and see if we can make one more stop before heading back to my parents." I noticed a place on Main Street in Endicott. "Let's stop there quick. I know right where it is."

Growing up, I had always remembered seeing Endicott Artistic Memorial Company right along Main Street. You really couldn't miss it. Conveniently located right across the street from a very large cemetery.

We pulled into a parking space facing the front of the small building. To the right of the building was an outdoor area filled with stone monuments, large to small, fancy to basic, and stone colors from light rose to jet black. Some looked to have just been delivered while others looked to be on display. We pulled the door open and were immediately greeted.

A man with a friendly smile told us his name was Dave and asked how he could help us. We told him we needed to inquire about a headstone. We explained to Dave about our loss.

"I'm very sorry," he said. I could sense his empathy.

We told him we were trying to figure out how much this would cost and get ideas on exactly what the headstone should look like. We handed him the sheet Dennis had given us, explaining it had all the requirements for a marker.

"You do know that your plot must be paid in full prior to getting a headstone, right?" he asked.

"Yes, we know that," Steve replied.

"Why don't you both grab a seat and I will go over a few options that I think you might like and give you an idea on cost and timetable."

He took out a small piece of white paper and started to draw a few different things. He sketched out a small angel and then a large cross with some ivy wrapped around it. "These are just a few ideas," he said. It was too early for me to think about this. All I knew was that he was kind and patient with us, and I wanted to give him our business.

Dave suggested we go outside and look at colors just to get some idea of stone choices and sizes.

We stood outside as Dave went over the stone types and colors. We headed back in while he wrote all the different prices down, and we agreed that when we paid for the plot in full, we would be back for the headstone.

"Thank you so much for your kindness," I said to him.

We took the small piece of white paper he had written on, shook his hand and left.

Sympathy From Friends

Back at my parents' house several beautiful bouquets of flowers and cards had arrived from friends and family.

People called, and I answered, but each time I got on the phone to speak, nothing would come out. I listened, thanked everyone who called, and hung up immediately. Everyone was supportive, even taking care of the details that I couldn't manage.

"I called Grace Episcopal earlier to see if Reverend Suriner could help with the burial service. She is no longer there," my mom said with concern.

It would have been nice to have Reverend Suriner present, as she was the one who married Steve and me. We had met with her on several occasions prior to our wedding day to discuss topics relating to married life and the expectations we had. I was glad that we had discussed all these topics openly as it would help "down the line," according to Reverend Suriner. One such topic was what religion our children would be baptized in. We both agreed to meet in the middle and that we would choose to have our children baptized Episcopal and attend an Episcopal Church.

We had decided to have the funeral at the cemetery on December 27. The weather was mild enough that cemetery workers were able to dig the plot we had just purchased and have the burial. We would have family and a few close friends attend.

"I will try to call the Lutheran church to see if someone can attend. I think with the holiday it's going to be tough to find someone," my mom said.

Steve's mom called the church Steve attended as a child to see if the priest could also be present at the burial.

My brother had stayed north since flying in on the 21st. My sister-in-law, Annalise, had flown in with my nephew Tyler for the burial. I asked our good friends Jackie and Mike, along with my best friend Lisa, to be with Steve and me at the burial. My other best friend, Erika, was on her honeymoon and had no idea what had even happened.

I spent the next few days in a complete fog, oftentimes staring at the Christmas tree for hours at a time, almost unaware of what was going on around me. It was nice to have my brother and his family there. My godson, Tyler, who was just two years old, helped distract me from my grief. He had no idea what had happened and was happy to be north with us. I found it refreshing to go outside with him and observe the awe in his eyes while he watched snowflakes fall from the sky for the very first time. He was the light for me those few dark days, and when I was with him, the pain of losing Jenny seemed just a little less sharp.

See You Again

I'd had a restless night, dreading what lay ahead. The morning was bitter cold with a dusting of snow on the ground and trees. Steve pulled into the cemetery and around the perimeter to the plot we had picked out. Waiting for us was the minister my mom had called from the church we attended when I was young. We sat in the car until everyone arrived. I looked around at the cars and the exhaust coming from the rear of each car, shrouding the entire area in fog.

"Are you going to be okay?" Steve asked, leaning toward me in the front seat of our car.

"I will," I whispered, as I began to cry. But I was not okay.

Since childhood, I had been the person who planned carefully and worked methodically toward my goals. I liked being in control of my life and orchestrating each step of my journey. Now, as I absorbed the reality of why we were standing at a gravesite on a freezing morning two days after Christmas, I felt overwhelmed. Steve and I had planned on starting our family, and we were excited to welcome our first baby in the coming year. Instead, we were preparing to bury her.

I took some deep breaths, tried to think of something other than what was happening and pulled the handle on the car door. I stepped out of the heated car into the cold. I shuddered at the little pile of dirt next to the freshly dug grave.

Frozen grass crunched beneath my shoes as I walked toward the casket. I watched as our family members and close friends walked up to the plot. They all had their eyes downcast and, with all conversation halted, an eerie silence surrounded our sad little group of mourners.

The minister had arrived a little early and was standing next to the casket holding a Bible in his gloved hands. He walked toward me and took my hand. I could barely make eye contact with him as I stared at the frozen ground.

"I'm very sorry for your loss," he said. I had heard those same words dozens of times already, and I was to hear them many more times in weeks to come. It is what we say to one another when nothing else seems possible. The sincerity of his words did give me a breath of comfort. As he turned away, I calmly took my hand and placed it in my coat pocket for warmth.

I could find no warmth, however, and the chill increased as I looked down and saw a tiny casket. The horror of knowing my beautiful Jenny was in that box was only somewhat lightened by the thought that I would someday lie with her for eternity. Knowing that we would be together gave me some peace.

As we stood silently together, the clouds cleared, and the sun shone down on us. I looked up into the brightening sky and believed it was a sign of hope for me. I felt the warmth of the sun on my face and believed that it was God's way of telling me to have faith. Steve glanced at me as if to ask what we were waiting for. His mother must have caught the look.

"We are just waiting on the priest. He should be here shortly," she said. It seemed disrespectful that he would be late.

We waited another few minutes. I was getting anxious and annoyed. This was hard on everyone, and I wished there was some way to help my family and friends feel more comfortable in this inherently uncomfortable situation. When he finally arrived, the ceremony, led jointly by the Catholic priest and the Lutheran minister, began.

The committal service was important to Steve and me. I wanted to pay attention and remember every verse that was read and every word that was offered for Jenny. As I listened, I felt disconcerted by what I heard.

Did he just call her Penny? I asked myself. Am I hearing things? I wasn't. The priest kept calling Jenny, Penny. Each time he said it felt like a knife in my gut; I wanted to scream my baby's name into the air. And the really strange part is that no one bothered to correct him.

"Her name is Jenny," I whispered with a sense of urgency to Steve. Hot tears of anger spilled from my eyes.

"He keeps calling her Penny. He keeps calling her Penny," I said again, even louder.

Isn't anyone going to correct him? He shows up late and now can't even get her name right? I was angry about the name, and I was also angry that he was distracting me from this vital moment.

"What an idiot," I murmured under my breath. Still, nothing was said.

At the conclusion of the ceremony, my mom handed out pink roses to everyone so they could each place one on top of Jenny's little casket.

As the pink roses were piled up one by one, I found enough strength to thank the minister.

"God bless you and keep you," he said as he shook my hand.

When I turned back, I saw that Jenny's little casket was covered in pretty pink roses. I placed the last one, forced myself to turn, and walked back toward the car, reluctant to leave, yet knowing the time had come to return to my parents' home and try to express my gratitude to everyone.

"We'll see you back at the house," my mom said, as she and my dad hugged me.

We all got into our cars and drove away from Jenny. I was exhausted.

Should Auld Acquaintance Be Forgot

Steve and I returned home with Maude Lilly a few days later. Life was moving in slow motion. The days seemed long, but in reality, my whole life had changed at warp speed. It had been over a week since Jenny had been born. Christmas had come and gone in a blur of sorrow, and we had buried our infant just a few days after. Now, we were leaving 2002 behind and turning the page to a new year. It didn't make me feel any different or better. We were just moving one numerical digit forward. Who really cared? I wondered.

With nothing to celebrate, we spent New Year's Eve with just the two of us. We didn't do anything special. I rested while Steve tried to get caught up on computer work. It was eerily quiet in the house and it bothered me. The next day was the same, and as we prepared for bed, Steve surprised me by announcing he was going to try to resume normal activities.

"I'm going to go to the office tomorrow," he said.

I was on leave for six weeks. I didn't even want to think about going back to work and facing the questions and the pity. I had no idea which of the physicians I called on regularly knew what had happened and which ones had not heard of my loss. I didn't want to have to relive everything over and over again until I cycled through all my offices. So, on Jan.2, I lay in bed while Steve went off to work.

The house was quiet for the first time since this all started back on December 20. Maude Lilly snuggled in with me. She sensed my sorrow. I stared at the Christmas tree in our bedroom. I thought about how when I put it up in early December, I was looking forward to the warmth, to the family fun, to the festive air of the holidays. I would have never imagined what was to come. The lights became blurry as I lay there and cried. Maude, sensing my sadness, tried to lick my tears away.

"Oh girl, I have to make it through this," I said, as she stared at me with her big brown eyes.

I knew that I needed to get up and get myself going. I needed to shower and try to resume some routines of a normal life. But I couldn't move. I have to get out of this bed, I said in my mind. I can't just lay here all day. I threw the covers off and sat on the edge of the bed. I needed to do something, anything. I felt my feet hit the floor and decided I would shower. Hot water pouring over my skin revitalized my body, but my mind was still clouded.

I dried off, ran a comb through my hair and threw on sweats and a sweatshirt before going downstairs. The quiet was eerie and uncomfortable. I paced around the house and stood for a moment looking out my sunroom windows. The monochrome winter scene matched my mood, and I turned to Maude, who was always by my side.

"What will we do today?" I said to Maude.

She jumped up with her front paws to say she was with me. I petted her and headed to the pile of mail sitting on my counter. I hadn't touched the mail or bills since this all began. I was amazed at the outpouring of love in my loss. I received some of the most touching cards and notes from friends, family, co-workers, and even a co-worker of Steve's in Rochester who had a stillborn baby, too.

On the other hand, as time went on, I was surprised by how many people didn't say anything. A few acted as if nothing had happened. Some just avoided me and the entire subject all together. Perhaps it was because, given the sadness of the situation, they didn't know what to say or maybe even how to say it. The death of a child in utero is a taboo topic, one we don't know how to talk about. I understood.

Follow-up And Test Results

It felt like déjà vu driving on Route 690. The sun was shining through the window of my Ford Taurus as I passed the empty State Fairgrounds to my right just as I had back on December 20. Everything may have looked the same on the outside, but the reality was that nothing was the same.

"I'm dreading this," I said aloud, even though I was alone in the car.

It would be the first time I would see Dr. Randolph since he returned from his vacation. So much had happened in the past couple of weeks. I had gone from thinking I was progressing with a successful pregnancy to learning that this pregnancy would not turn out the way I thought it would; we had birth, death, burial, and now mourning. Arriving at the Heritage Landing office, I found a parking spot and turned off the engine.

I took a few deep breaths as I lingered in my car outside the office. It had taken resolve to turn the car off, and I was unsure if I was going to be able to get out and go into the office. I knew I shouldn't be late, so I forced myself to do what was expected of me.

It felt like everyone was staring at me as I opened the door and walked in. I checked in with Karen at the window. She immediately came out and gave me a hug. My heart was racing and I could feel myself welling up. I was grateful when Dr. Randolph's nurse, Lori, took me from the waiting area. She walked beside me and closed the door behind us.

"Hi Jenny," Lori said as she gave me a hug. "Let's go back to Dr. Randolph's office." On the way, she asked a routine question, but she did so with sincere interest.

"How are you doing?" Lori asked. I replied automatically, as I had so many times in the preceding days.

"I'm okay," I said as my voice cracked.

I was grateful for Lori. She was a genuine person. About as tall as I, light brown hair and pretty blue eyes. She was a mom with grown children. I remember when she told me the ages of her kids and how old she was when she had them. She certainly didn't look her age. I remember thinking when we spoke about her having kids at a younger age thinking that maybe I had waited too long. I felt vulnerable having gone through this loss, and Lori was one of the people who really made me feel cared for.

She asked about my physical healing, and I told her the worst had been becoming engorged. It was my fault, I admitted. I didn't hear the nurse giving me all the discharge instructions when I left the hospital, and I never opened and looked at the discharge papers once I got home.

Then, Lori asked about how I was feeling emotionally. I explained to her that I thought I was doing okay and was asked in the hospital if I wanted to take some prescription drugs to help me with the emotional toll this was taking on me. I had declined any drugs as I felt that for me it was important to try and work through the feelings. The doctor had also mentioned going to some sort of counseling or support group if that was something I might find helpful. But, as is my habit, I wanted to work through the grief myself.

With a soft knock on the door, Dr. Randolph entered, and I felt relieved to see him again. He shook my hand and smiled before he sat across from me. He was tan from his vacation. His smile was warm and genuine but, today, it seemed to express his sorrow. His brown eyes showed his concern.

After greeting me, Dr. Randolph asked the question everyone asked me now: "How are you doing?"

For the second time in just a few minutes, I gave the automatic response I had become so used to.

"I'm okay, I guess, under the circumstances." I didn't know how to respond in any other way. Could I possibly say I was broken in ways that I know will never be mended and that I am sorrowful every minute of every day? No. So I say, I'm okay.

He said he was sorry not to have been here for me and that he was sorry for our loss.

I could sense his sincere sadness. He knew it had been hard for me to have a physician that I did not know deliver Jenny. I understood and assured him I did not have any hard feelings. But I felt enormous relief that he was with me now and I knew I was in good hands going forward. I trusted him.

Dr. Randolph explained that any time there is something that happens with a pregnancy such as mine, it is important to try to understand why it happened and how to make sure it doesn't happen again. He also made it a point to say that sometimes there is no answer or explanation for a loss like this. Even though we are always looking for a reason or explanation, there may not be one and this can be difficult to understand and, more importantly, accept. He said he was aware that we decided to have an autopsy on the baby and that it must have been a difficult decision.

I told him that at first, I didn’t want to have it done; however, the more I thought about it, the more I wanted to know if my daughter's death was something that could be explained. He expressed that he was hopeful we would have some sort of explanation for what happened. I was looking for an answer and was hopeful he could give me one. Deep down in the back of my mind, I feared that there would be some sort of test result that would indicate that I may not be able to physically carry a child full term. It weighed heavily on me.

Dr. Randolph wanted to go over the lab tests done upon my arrival at the hospital. He opened a large manila file folder and began leafing through it. He pulled out several pieces of white paper and turned them toward me on his desk. I could see his initials and date next to everything showing that he had previously reviewed the data and when.

He started by mentioning that a complete blood panel was done, and it all looked good. Nothing was flagged or stood out as unusual. On top of the traditional testing several other tests were completed. An ANA screen test is a blood test that looks for antinuclear antibodies in your system. This came back negative. If it were positive, it might indicate that there may be an underlying autoimmune process that affects the development of the placenta and can lead to early pregnancy loss. A CMV IgG test, which is a valuable tool for diagnosing primary Cytomegalovirus infection during pregnancy, was completed and showed negative.

Dr. Randolph continued to relay important details. He told me that low avidity indicates primary infection within the preceding 3 to 4 months, with an increased risk of intrauterine transmission to the fetus/newborn. The value was less than 4 which is considered negative. The Toxoplasma IgM test came back negative. This would show an early infection during the period of pregnancy, or it may be a reflection of past infections that occurred a few months before pregnancy. A cardiolipin blood test was also done. They do this in women who have had miscarriage to double check for abnormal blood clotting or bleeding. Sometimes, women have an autoimmune problem and the cardiolipin antibodies show up in their blood. This was all negative. The Parvo B19 test was also negative. This could have shown an infection within the last 7 to 120 days.

Sitting there, I was overwhelmed with the details. He told me the last test done was for the Coxsackie virus. Coxsackie virus is one type of virus known as enteroviruses. They are highly contagious. These viruses can pass from person to person on unwashed hands and contaminated surfaces. They can also spread through droplets of fluid sprayed into the air when an infected person sneezes or coughs.

"When I looked at the test results, I realized you had an elevated titer count," Dr. Randolph said. A titer count measures the presence and number of antibodies in the blood. A higher titer count may indicate recent infection. Dr. Randolph had circled the results on the white paper.

"It appears the lab work showed that you and the baby had Coxsackie B virus," he said. I looked at Dr. Randolph with a blank stare. He went on to explain there are 6 types and typically many people are immune to the virus as often you are exposed to the virus as a child or in your younger years.

Coxsackie B virus is one of the most common viral causes for stillbirth or can lead to medical issues in a newborn that can be life-threatening.

"According to the report," he said, "your titer level was 1:640 for the Coxsackie B Type 4 virus. 1:10 to 1:40 could represent immunity or low titers present early in the course of infection. But 1:80 or greater in a single serum suggests current or recent infection." My count was extremely high, indicating that I, along with my baby, had most likely been infected.

Dr. Randolph explained that while we aren't certain this is the cause, it is something. He seemed a bit relieved to have some sort of medical explanation for my loss. I couldn't help but let my mind wander as I wondered how I contracted this virus. Maybe it was in one of the hospitals or doctor's offices I called on, or perhaps just being in the general public.

Dr. Randolph reassured me that everything else I was tested for looked great. This appeared to be the only explanation given the lab work that was done. He reassured me that this information doesn't make what happened any easier; however, he said, it helps to try and understand what the cause of death might have been.

I asked him if there was any other additional testing he would recommend having done. He told me about a physician, Dr. Scott Sander, based out of

Rochester, and that he felt I should consult with him. Dr. Randolph said he had spoken with Dr. Connor, who had delivered baby Jenny, and that they both agreed this would be the right steps to take. Dr. Sander is part of a large OB/GYN group, and Dr. Randolph said they are fantastic at what they do.

"Both Dr. Connor and I feel it's important to consult over these findings and see what other genetic/lab testing he might want to do," Dr. Randolph said. He said by taking these steps we could cross all our T's and dot all our I's. "By doing so, when you are ready to try again, you will be able to make an informed decision." Dr. Randolph and I both agreed to go this route. I wanted to make sure we were not missing anything. The more data, the better. We should be able to uncover something if it is there. He said Dr. Sander and his group are familiar with dealing with high-risk pregnancies, and they have the resources to conduct further testing through Strong Memorial Hospital.

I nodded my head in agreement as he stood up and, once again, we shook hands.

Dr. Randolph said Lori would make a call to the Rochester office and take care of scheduling. "We will get through this. Just take care of yourself and I will look forward to seeing you after all the testing is completed," Dr. Randolph said as he left.

I stood up from the chair and went to the check-out window.

Lori came out and confirmed she would call me with the appointment in Rochester.

I wasn't sure how I felt when I left the office. I was still overwhelmed by the situation and, even though it looked like we had an answer as to why baby Jenny had died, I still felt unsure about my ability to actually have a baby. I knew I needed to go home and research this virus so that I could understand it better for myself. There was so much in front of me. I did feel good about how Dr. Randolph explained to me that both he and Dr. Connor felt it was important to cover all our bases before moving forward. I knew one thing for sure: I could not endure a loss like this ever again.

Second Thoughts

Over the days that followed, I had some time to rest and try to heal physically and emotionally. There were moments in the quiet that made me want to return to work immediately. Steve had gone back to work and the house was quiet. The quiet bothered me as it left me with my emotions which seemed to vary depending on the day. A busy mind would have been a break from the utter sadness and loss I had experienced. I tried to understand the changes my body was experiencing from a healing perspective. My hormones were most likely completely out of balance. I wondered if I should just get back to work; however, at the same time I was unsure how to handle the emotional rollercoaster I was on.

My job entailed calling on individual physician offices, along with institutions such as hospitals, psychiatric centers, and even a maximum-security prison, to promote my pharmaceutical product line. I had established great rapport with most of my physicians and office staff who knew me well enough to know that I had become pregnant. This made me feel torn about when I would return within that six-week grace period. Having a busy work mind meant keeping my mind from wandering back to the dark hole I found myself in the days after delivering Jenny. It was this delicate balance of trying to move forward but move forward in a healthy emotional and physical way. In reality, my hormones were trying to level out while my body was still trying to physically heal and process the loss of a baby.

I went for my four-week checkup with Dr. Randolph. We both talked about how my body would take some time to heal physically and how the emotional part of what I had experienced would take time. He acknowledged the difficulty long term in dealing with such a personal loss. He asked if I had sought out counseling or a support group. I did tell him I spoke with another woman on the phone who had experienced the same loss, but I didn't feel it was helpful for me. I told him that a support group didn't sound like something I would find helpful. I was never one to speak in an open forum about my feelings and tended to always keep my feelings to myself. I knew myself enough that I would not find this type of environment helpful.

"Just don't keep it all bottled up inside," he said.

I know he was concerned for my mental well being and wanted me to be able to move forward in a healthy manner. I told him that I felt I was ready to get back to work even though I had another two weeks until I was required to return. From a physical standpoint, he gave me the clear to go ahead and return if I felt I was ready. When I left his office that morning, I made the decision that it was time to move forward and get back to life as I knew it.

I called my boss Jack. "When do you think you will be coming back to work?" my boss asked on the other end of the phone.

"I think I am ready. I would like to come back next Monday. Do you know if Gary was able to speak to many of our physicians about what happened?" I asked. My boss explained that he and my co-worker had understood my concerns.

"I know Gary said he was trying to let as many people know as possible so you wouldn't have to explain every time you made a visit," he said. Then he promised to let Gary know I was planning on coming back.

As he spoke, I thought about Gary and our relationship as counterparts over the past couple of years. We were different in many ways while being similar in others–the perfect balance for collegial partners. We both worked hard, were overachievers and cared deeply about our mission of helping people. Deep down we were two caring individuals who felt incredibly touched by many of the patient stories our physicians would share with us. We witnessed firsthand as we called on our institutions and individual offices the struggle of mental illness on not only the individual, but also the family unit. We both would often talk about how hard it was to witness this. Gary always provided me with wonderful words of wisdom, and I appreciated his optimism, life experience, and wisdom. I enjoyed talking with him about his deep commitment to his Jewish faith, his family, and his hopes for retirement with his wife. Gary would always insist that in every circumstance, "It's always about family." He was right. I focused again on the reason for my call.

"So my plan is to return next Monday," I said, trying to convey a confidence I didn't fully feel. "I will make sure to call HR after we hang up. I'll also email them with my intention to return to the field. How does that sound?" I asked.

"Sounds good, Jenny," Jack replied.

I knew I needed to go back to work. My company had given me some time and allowed me up to six weeks if I needed it. The thought of having to go back into all the doctor's offices and hospitals and face everyone was overwhelming. It was something I really dreaded. I wanted to avoid those confrontations so much that I began to contemplate looking for a different job and actually not returning to the job I had worked so hard to establish myself in before the trauma of December. I decided to discuss my feelings about my career with Steve, hoping that he'd understand my consternation.

"I don't know if I can go back to my job," I said that evening.

"What do you mean?" Steve was surprised at my announcement. I realized his situation was different from mine. He returned to his office after Jenny's funeral, made a few explanations, and moved forward. I had to contemplate the possibility of a series of questions, explanations, and expressions of sympathy. It would be uncomfortable for everyone.

"I am hesitant about seeing all of my physicians and having to explain everything if they are not aware of what happened to us," I said. "Steve, I have been thinking that they all knew I was pregnant. How many times do you think I can face the question about whether we have a baby boy or girl? I just don't want to deal with it. There is a part of me that just wants a fresh start. No questions."

Steve took a minute to process what I was saying. I had the feeling he didn't fully grasp my hesitations. He said he understood that I had to do what I felt was right.

"I understand what you are saying. But, Jenny, think about if you get a new job and then if you decide you want to go forward and have a baby," he said. "Imagine the stress of a new job along with trying to have a successful pregnancy." Steve saw the situation in only practical terms.

"Stay the course with work. It's what you know and what you're great at," he said.

"I know, it just feels overwhelming." I felt he dismissed my concerns, and it made me sad.

I knew Steve was right. I spoke to my mom and dad about it, too. They agreed with Steve. As hard as it was going to be, I accepted that I needed to just work through it. I knew that after the weeks of calling on all my offices and institutions, I would be in the clear. Four more weeks of having to potentially talk about my misfortune.

I took the same mindset as I had when I left the hospital. I have to feel the uncomfortable moments and work through them. No drugs, no numbing. This was what was best long term.

Back to Work

I stood in front of the mirror. I was still wearing my maternity suit as I couldn't fit into anything else. I threw a bright, patterned silk blouse on to make me feel and look brighter. This was harder than I imagined it would be. Up until this point, I hadn't even thought about the pregnancy weight. It wasn't until today, when I went to throw on my pre-pregnancy suit, that it hit me. I couldn't even get the pants over my thighs. I was reminded that the pregnancy weight was still with me even though I had no child to show for it. I sat on the bed. I looked over at Maude as she lay sleeping on my pillows. I wanted to crawl back into bed and hope all my sorrow and solicitude would go away. At the moment, I wasn't sure if I was actually going to make it to work.

Pulling myself together I headed back into the bathroom, did my makeup and hair. I convinced myself that if I could just make a few calls today and deal with whatever came up, that I would have at least made a start into returning to my career. That's what I'll do, I said to myself. I'll get in the car, go to a few offices, and call it a day. I continued giving myself pep talks all the way to my first call.

Arriving, I sat outside in the parking lot of my first office instead of jumping out of the car and striding into the building as I had in the past. I reminded myself to work through all these feelings and keep moving forward. Having pushed through the first difficult situation, the days and weeks that followed were challenging, but also good at the same time. There were physicians who had no idea what I had experienced, ones that knew and greeted me with a caring heart, and a few who thought I had a healthy baby and wondered if I had been blessed with a boy or a girl. For the most part, though, I was able to resume work, and it was good to mentally concentrate on doing my job instead of thinking about all that I had been through.

It had been about a month since I had returned to the field. I received a phone call from Jack letting me know I was on his schedule for a two-day ride along. Many of us pharma field reps always talked about the dreaded ride. It really depended on how you felt about your boss. I never really seemed to mind the ride along. For the most part, I always had my ducks in a row and had worked hard and I wanted my manager to see my hard work paying off. This time it was different. I had these feelings toward Jack that were bottled up. I found his actions completely insensitive. I really didn't want to work for someone like him. I wasn't sure how I was going to handle the few days together. I had cycled through all my offices so there were no uncomfortable situations to deal with having to explain about the loss of my child. It festered within me though, and that was also a reason I became torn about returning to work. I decided that I was going to have to speak to Jack directly about how he made me feel. I was always of the mindset that difficult conversations many times are the only way to speak your truth and set yourself free. Otherwise, these feelings left unsaid will only weigh on you. And so I knew when the moment was right on our two-day ride along, I would have a direct conversation with him to address these feelings.

As we sat at a Thai restaurant we liked on Erie Boulevard, where we often talked about how we were both headed up the corporate ladder, I knew this would be the appropriate time to unpack these negative feelings I had toward him.

Jack was about ten years older than I. He was a slim-built man with a mustache that made him look a bit like Groucho Marx from the 1930s. You could tell he was never an athlete but more of the studious, quiet type. He never seemed to get too excited about much, and his personality and voice were always pitched at a steady monotone. He didn't fit the typical profile of a sales representative, let alone a manager.

Despite our differences in character, we got along. We were both driven in the sales arena, and he was always happy when we would have a good productive sales day together. We often talked openly about other offers from competitors and other companies along the way. But we agreed we were happy in our current roles and with the company. The grass isn't always greener on the other side, we would profess. When I would share with him that I did have another offer on the table and felt like I was wavering a bit, he would always make me think twice about making the switch by providing me stock options, a few additional days of vacation, or a pay increase.

After ordering, I felt it was the appropriate time to speak openly.

"I didn't appreciate how you made me feel when I took the Family Medical Leave Act and the difficult time you gave me when I would have to call in sick," I said as I stared directly at Jack.

He became red in the face. I could tell by his body language he felt uncomfortable. I did not say anything else allowing him the chance to respond. He was quiet for a few moments. I know he sensed my disappointment in him. Then, he expressed his regret in the only way possible.

"I'm sorry I made you feel that way," he said.

Perhaps he did feel sorry, but his reluctance to accommodate my unexpected unique circumstances was a side I saw in him that I wouldn't have known existed. To that point, we always got along great. All I could think of to explain his insensitivity was that since my performance contributed to his all-around success and income, he wanted me in the field selling. He certainly did not want me at home sick or on leave. Perhaps, I considered, I really didn't know him. And if this was indeed the reason, we weren't anything alike. Overall, I had built up a bit of resentment toward him since his refusal to accommodate my wellness needs. He gave me a difficult time when I made the decision to take family medical leave for a few weeks early in my pregnancy to get myself through the first trimester. He also made it a point to give me a hard time over the phone each time I would call in sick for doctor's appointments during the pregnancy. He would ask that if the doctor's office had appointments on a Saturday, that would be preferred. So, when I lost baby Jenny and he sent me a huge bouquet of beautiful flowers expressing his sympathy, I simply walked them out to my garbage can and tossed them in. Completely out of character for me, as I was truly appreciative for all the kind thoughts, cards, messages, and prayers family, friends, and coworkers sent. Indeed, flowers have always been one of my favorite things in life and when I did receive a bouquet for a special occasion, I was deeply grateful and enjoyed them tremendously. I often say to my family that when I read an obituary that states "in lieu of flowers," it always disappoints me for some reason. To me, flowers are a traditional way to symbolize big life events. We send them or give them for all kinds of reasons. Birthdays, holidays, weddings, and even to acknowledge the passing of someone. All these big life moments. I hope that my family will keep with the tradition. Shower me with as many as possible. This beautiful bouquet deserved to be enjoyed; however, the sender behind it took away from any of the beauty the flowers possessed.

I took the next day off of work as a personal day. Jack probably thought I was going for an interview for another company after our lunch together. I had decided I would no longer share any of my personal life with Jack and from now on, it was strictly work business.

I wasn't sure exactly where Dr. Sander's office was in Rochester. I had googled it and it looked to be about an hour and twenty minutes from my home in Baldwinsville. I was feeling anxious but excited at the same time. I wanted to get to this appointment and keep moving forward. In my mind it was all about forward momentum. I pulled out of my driveway in the early morning and headed to the New York State Thruway. I was thankful the weather gods had cooperated for me. You never know what you're going to get weather-wise in Upstate New York between October and April. Today, it was mid-March and an overcast cold day. No snow. Perfect. I listened to talk radio to try and keep my mind off of what was ahead of me. Too much thinking about the uncertainty seemed to get the better of me. I traveled along the Thruway until picking up Route 390, then took exit 16A and made my way to the office address Lori had given me. I pulled up to the large, older-looking brick building with black shutters in an office park not too far off the Thruway. I made it.

In the exam room, I took off my pants and underwear, put my disposable gown on, and sat on the examining table while the paper crunched underneath me. That sound brought me back to the moment in Dr. Randolph's office when they were looking for the baby's heartbeat. My heart started to race. I took a few deep breaths and tried to focus on my visit. I was doing this to learn, to gather every bit of information possible about the cause of Jenny's death and my chances for carrying a baby full term in the future. I needed answers. I heard the knock on the door that meant the doctor was coming in.

"Hi Jenny, I'm Dr. Sander," He reached out his arm and we shook hands. "It's really nice to meet you," he said, welcoming me to what I hoped would be a thorough process of scientific exploration.

A slight man with glasses, he spoke with assurance, and I immediately felt confident in him. He expressed his sympathy for my loss and asked how I was feeling. As usual, I gave the automatic response that I was doing okay. He held a folder in his hand and raised it as he said he had taken the time to look through all the testing that was done both on me and baby Jenny. He agreed that it looked as though the Coxsackie B virus could be the explanation of my daughter's death.

Dr. Sander explained that this practice had the resources to do some additional lab tests. This would allow us to take a deeper dive into reasons why my pregnancy ended as it had. It also would help us understand if there could be an underlying condition I was not aware of that might prevent me from carrying a child full term. He explained that the problem didn't lie with getting pregnant, which for some women can be an issue, but with trying to understand the ability for me to carry a healthy baby full term. He asked me about my experience with severe nausea and vomiting early in my pregnancies along with my general feeling of unwellness. I explained to him that I had suffered an early miscarriage prior to getting pregnant with Jenny, and I knew I was pregnant each time because it was like a switch had been flipped within me. I went from feeling fine, as I always had, to feeling sick. I had no energy, I vomited frequently, and it reminded me of when I had the flu a few times earlier in my life. He explained that he wanted to make sure my body was not signaling that there is a problem and this feeling of unwellness was the sign.

"There can be circumstances when a woman's body wants to reject a pregnancy," Dr. Sander said. "I want to make sure this is not the case with you, Jenny. Let's start with an exam and then talk about what types of lab work I would like to have done." My mind was reeling in fear that I might be one of those women he described that is incapable of carrying a child.

He called his nurse into the room while he instructed me to inch down to the bottom of the table so he could conduct an examination.

"Everything looks good," the doctor said, as he put a sample in a vial from the examination. He stepped out of the room as his nurse helped me inch back up on the table and instructed me to get dressed.

I threw my pants back on, glad to be in my own clothes again, and waited for the doctor to come back into the room. There was a knock at the door. I paid close attention to everything Dr. Sander told me.

"I am going to set up a lab appointment at Strong Memorial Hospital next week for you," he began. "We are going to test for a few things you haven't been tested for and a few you have already been tested for. I would like to repeat them just for comparison." He listed the lab work expected: A regular TSH level, a lupus anticoagulant, Antithrombin 3 assay, protein C and S along with an F-5 Leiden/PT.

"Having these done will give us an even better look into anything that might be going on with you regarding pregnancy. I will then review the results with Dr. Randolph, since he is your attending physician, and we can go from there. Does that sound like a plan?' Dr. Sander asked.

"Sounds good," I said. I was encouraged by his thoroughness and his careful explanations.

“Keep your spirits up, Jenny. I really think you are going to be okay. Let’s just do these last few tests to give us all the confidence we need going forward. Especially you,” the doctor said. He assured me that when he received the results, he would have me come back to review them.

“I will also consult with Dr. Randolph, as I can imagine this is weighing heavy on you. I’m sorry you have had to go through this,” he said.

“Thank you," I whispered as I welled up with tears at his kindness.

I walked to the parking lot, got into the car, took a deep breath, and headed back to Baldwinsville.

Rochester Redux

A week later, I drove west on the New York State Thruway to Strong Memorial Hospital again, this time for my lab appointment. It was March 24. I wasn't sure what to expect but knew this was me making progress toward my goal of one day becoming a mom. I pulled into the large parking ramp at the hospital and found a spot. I decided to sit in the car for a few minutes before going inside.

I took a few deep breaths and walked through the automated sliding doors. This was a busy place. And the scent! I have never been able to get over the aroma all hospitals have: the disinfectant colliding with bodily fluids. I held my breath on and off, as I always did, until my nose could adjust. I searched for a directory and found my way to the hospital lab. It was crowded with people who appeared either bored or anxious. I heard last names being called frequently, and there was a flurry of people coming and going. The waiting room was a large rectangle with blue faux-leather seats around the perimeter and a double row situated along the center. The tile floor was a shiny cream color. From a decorating point of view, sterile with a hint of blue. I had come to the conclusion over the years of calling on offices and institutions that all these places must use the same interior decorating firm. The receptionist slid the glass window open as she asked for my name and ID. Insurance card, too. I handed her the paperwork from my visit with Dr. Sander along with my insurance card.

After she scanned my insurance card and looked at my license, she handed both back and told me to take a seat. I took one of the few open chairs, a seat in the corner, but it wasn't long before an older woman called my name. I quickly stood up and walked toward her. I was nervous about what was to come, my hands sweating.

"We are going to be taking quite a bit of blood work. Just relax and let me know if you begin to experience any kind of lightheadedness," the woman said kindly.

Not knowing of my circumstances, she started to question why I was there. Perhaps she thought I was having trouble getting pregnant. I took a deep breath and explained the basics of my situation. She looked at me and was silent for a moment.

"I'm sorry for your loss," she said as I, once again, welled up with tears.

I expressed to her my hopes of becoming a mom someday and that getting this blood work done would surely help me get there. I tried to put a positive note on our conversation as I knew she felt bad for upsetting me. I tried hard to focus myself on something other than the feeling of wanting to weep.

She pushed the needle into the vein while holding several vials in her other hand.

"Are you doing okay?" she asked.

"I'm doing fine," I replied, grateful for the technique of this skilled phlebotomist. She applied some pressure to my arm as she took out the needle and put some cotton and tape on it.

"Leave this on for a bit. Then in about an hour take it off. You're all set, Jenny."

I got myself back out to the car, where I felt the need to process all the emotions of the day. I rested back against the headrest and took a deep breath as I held the steering wheel with both hands, just gathering strength for the drive home. I wasn't sure what this blood work would show, but I knew that this was a good thing that I had done. A car horn was blaring. It became more frequent. I realized then that a car was waiting to take my parking spot on the ramp. I quickly started the car, threw it into reverse, exited the parking ramp, and headed back to Baldwinsville.

The weeks came and went. In early April, I could hear the geese call upon their return. I stepped out my front door and looked up. Hundreds of them flying overhead. I had said goodbye to them in late fall with all the hopes and dreams of having a baby in my arms when I stepped outside to welcome them upon their return. Little did I know then what

I knew now. It made me sad and hopeful at the same time.

I followed up with Dr. Sander on May 26, two months since my initial visit. After the preliminary intake, a nurse ushered me into his office. When he came in, I stood, and we shook hands as we had the first time.

"Grab a seat," he said as he pulled the chair out for me.

My sense of uncertainty was overwhelming. My heart was pounding because I felt that this specific moment might change the trajectory of my entire life. I desperately wanted to have a child, and I couldn't help but fear that it might not be possible. I knew deep in my heart that such news would be tough for me to accept. Unsure of what the blood work had revealed and afraid of what he was about to tell me, I tried to cycle positive things through my mind. I still was having a hard time grasping what had happened to my infant daughter, even all these months later. I forced myself to focus, not wanting to miss a word of this talk, or misunderstand anything the doctor would say.

"I've had the chance to look at the testing you have completed," Dr. Sander announced. "I did go ahead and cross compare some of the results that were repeated along with the new testing that was done. I'm happy to say everything looks fantastic! There seems to be no indication of any issue with you being able to carry a child to full term. I would encourage you to try again."

The weight of what could have been instantly lifted from me. I had hope. Much needed hope. We could try again. There was no medical reason not to. I felt my shoulders relax and a smile spread across my face. Even the doctor seemed jubilant.

"I will follow up with Dr. Randolph. Do you have any questions for me? Jenny, go forward and try to have a baby. Send me a photo of the baby when you have him or her," he said. With the standard invitation to get in touch if I should need anything, Dr. Sander shook my hand and walked out ahead of me. I felt as if he had solved a major mystery, discovered a new planet, and broken the code to a lingering enigma.

I left the office with an internal sense of hope. I called my mom, Steve, anyone who was important in my life, and shared my good news. We could have a child. We could expand our little family.

Talk radio was replaced with music for the drive home. The weather was nice, and the sun shone down through the car windows. The uncertainty about being able to carry a child and be a mom had been lifted for the most part. I was still concerned; however, I was relying on all the medical tests and feedback from the doctors who had seen me to increase my confidence. Overall, I did feel a sense of lightness. I found myself daydreaming about what was to come. I wanted so much in my heart to become a mom. I dreamed of it, prayed for it, and counted on it.

As I drove along the Thruway, I wondered what it would be like to travel as a family. I had hoped to be able to travel back and forth to my parents during the winter months from Syracuse to southwest Florida. I anticipated fun days on the beach playing in the sand. Walking along the water looking for shells and spotting a few dolphins if we were lucky. And I envisioned simple times at home–like going for stroller walks with Maude Lilly by our side. We would enjoy perfect days doing all kinds of activities like playing in the yard, exploring new things, followed by a bath and book each night. And, when I did become a mom, that particular day would be etched in my heart forever, always to be celebrated with a big party to acknowledge the monumental moment in time. How I had always loved my birthday growing up. My mom always made my birthday special, and I had hoped to do the same for my children. A small party with the best part of every birthday: cake. It was always about the cake with me and still is. I looked forward to letting my children make the decision on what kind of cake they wanted and whether they wanted a party.

These visions of what life would be like made me feel happier than I had been in a long time. At last I knew that I could carry a child to term, that

Steve and I would have a chance to do all the things we'd talked about as we nurtured, taught, and–most of all–loved our children in the future.

Trying Again

I stood in front of the mirror. I could tell by the bags under my eyes and the pale look of my skin. The switch had flipped. All indications pointed to my being pregnant, but instead of reveling in happiness, I was filled with fear. Steve and I were going to be parents, and there was no turning back.

It was late June, and I was sitting back on the examining table at my OB/GYN's office. As I moved around, the paper made that all-too-familiar crunching sound that did nothing to calm my nerves.

"Congratulations, Jenny!" Lori said, as she gave me a big hug.

My estimated due date was February 27, 2004. I was experiencing all the same symptoms I did when I was pregnant with Jenny, and that left me uneasy. I was busy working and kept trying my best to keep up with my usual pace while, at the same time, tackling my pregnancy symptoms. I was scared to tell anyone other than family about the pregnancy, but I was forced to tell my boss. I needed him to understand why I could not function as I normally did.

I envied all the women who told me they felt radiant and energetic during pregnancy. I was happy for them, but my experience was far different. I had warnings from people I trusted most on this earth to protect my own health and give my baby the best chance possible of a full-term delivery.

"You need to focus on really taking it easy," Dr. Randolph said.

"I'm telling you, Jenny, you need to be very careful," my mom advised with concern after I shared that I was indeed pregnant again.

I knew all these things. I knew I should listen to my body.

"Mom, I am taking it as easy as I can. I have to work and will do the best I can," I said, annoyed.

"The job isn't important. You know that," she replied.

I looked at the days, weeks, and months that lay ahead, and I felt as if I was at the beginning of a marathon.

Dr. Randolph insisted I make some accommodations in my busy schedule, and that was what I planned on doing. My body was again resistant to my developing infant inside. I was hopeful that this time I would feel different, but I had nausea and illness, just as I had with Jenny.

I followed up with Dr. Randolph weekly. He was committed to trying to get me to the finish line and I knew by his actions he meant it. I was already struggling with trying to work and travel while dealing with the effects the pregnancy was having on my body.

I spoke to Dr. Randolph about trying to work at least half the day. This would allow me to try to get some work done while limping along and trying to get through. He thought it would be a good idea. He filled out some paperwork asking the company HR department people to decrease my work hours temporarily. He wanted me to work four hours a day until I could get through the first trimester. My doctor was supportive, but my boss was not.

"I know that you have submitted a written notice to the company from your doctor for four-hour workdays, Jenny," he said. "But I need to tell you that the company will not support such a schedule."

I was shocked. I couldn't fathom why they would not allow me to work at least four hours a day. It didn't make sense to me. Deep down I felt disappointed in how I was being made to feel.

I couldn't believe what I was hearing from my boss, Jack, on the other end of the phone. I had always had stellar job reviews, and I had a reputation for working incredibly hard. This was the last response I could have imagined. Jack was cold and matter-of-fact. What an asshole, I thought. In the back of my mind, I couldn't help but think that he was pissed because I would be out of my territory and not making the sales he needed in order to look good. He would miss the bonus money that came along with it. I thought I would be met with encouragement when it came to me trying to take care of myself and the baby I was carrying. This felt brutal, like some retaliation for my getting pregnant. I wasn't sure how I was going to handle it.

"I'm pissed," I said to Steve later that day.

I found myself angry that after Dr. Randolph had insisted on giving me a note to decrease my hours that my company stated to me that such a schedule was not available. I was in a huff over the entire situation as I continued to express my frustration to Steve.

"I'm not surprised," Steve said, speaking as a businessman himself. "You work in sales and you're good at what you do. They want you out there selling."

I called my mom and told her what was going on. She took an entirely different view of the company's refusal to accommodate my pregnancy needs.

"You are going to need to look into other options," she said.

I started to research what my other options might be, as I didn't want to leave my job. I liked my job and the people I worked with. I also enjoyed the offices and institutions I called on. From what I could find, it looked as though my only option to keep my job was to look into short-term disability.

At my next appointment, I spoke with Dr. Randolph about what had transpired. I explained my idea about taking short-term disability with my company so that I could focus on taking care of myself and the baby.

"If I start to feel better, I would like to return to work, but at the moment they are leaving me no other option than to take short-term disability," I said in frustration. Dr. Randolph then revealed the red tape that went along with that decision.

"I understand, Jenny. Please know they will require regular updates from me, and from my past experience, I know they will make it tough for you to be able to do this," he said. "I've been down this path before. Companies are very resistant to these requests."

"Really?" I said in disbelief.

"Yes. You would be surprised how terrible companies can be."

I spent the scheduled hour having the baby monitored. According to Dr. Randolph, everything was looking good. No stress on me or the baby. He detected a strong, level heartbeat from him or her. I was good to go until the next week.

I decided I would call my Corporate Health Services HR person as soon as I got home.

"Hi, this is Linda Brown," a voice said on the other end.

I said I was calling to inquire about my option of short-term disability. I explained that I was pregnant again and my physician recently put me on half workdays. I told her my boss had called me and said such a schedule would not be supported by the company. I told her I was sure she was aware of his call.

"First of all, congratulations," she said.

I explained to her that I had not been able to work a full day since July 14 and that I was committed to trying to have a successful pregnancy. I ended up having to take off June 30 to July 7, using up all my vacation days. I was inquiring about going on short-term disability and explained that I was given a half-day restriction note from my physician.

Linda informed me that Dr. Randolph would have to fill out a statement of Medical Condition. The company would then review it and make a decision on whether short-term disability would be approved or not. The company would then require the attending physician to provide initial and periodic statements regarding my diagnosis, treatment, and prognosis if the short-term disability is approved. I realized that what I was asking was a lot of extra work for Dr. Randolph and that maybe the company had instituted these procedures to discourage workers from seeking the disability option.

I wasn't sure how I was going to handle my boss. I felt as if he was trying to edge me out. I decided that speaking to him via phone would not be the best course of action, so I decided to send him any correspondence via email with HR copied. At this point, I was going to protect myself. I could see he wasn't in favor of me being out of territory, and I wanted to document our conversations.

I received a letter from HR regarding my approval for short-term disability benefits dated July 21, 2003. The letter detailed my request for a paid leave of absence pursuant to the pharmaceutical company's short-term disability policy and that it was approved. The letter was lengthy, and it detailed the very stringent deadlines and expectations that my provider must adhere to in order for me to remain eligible for my benefits.

Every week, my company hounded Dr. Randolph about my part-time disability status, and the HR representative continued to call me and question me as to when I thought I would be able to return to a full-time work schedule. I was both frustrated and disappointed with how I was being treated. I just wanted to honor my doctor's instructions and give myself the best possible chance of having a healthy baby. Was that so hard to understand?

I made the decision on August 18 to notify my company via email of my intent to resign. I felt strongly that if I didn't give up my job and focus solely on having a healthy baby, I may never be able to realize my dream of becoming a mom. The stress of my employment situation was adding to the stress of trying to have a healthy, full-term baby. The constant calls from HR inquiring about my status on returning to work full time and Dr. Randolph being hounded with weekly updates and inquiries were all too much. I felt forced out.

So after six successful and rewarding years with my company, I threw in the towel for the bigger reward.

I didn't feel any sense of relief after giving my official notice to resign. I actually felt angry that this decision seemed forced on me. After so many years of proving myself as a reliable, high achieving corporate worker, I was turning my back on my career, and I felt conflicted about the decision. But my family centered me by reinforcing what was to come: A healthy baby.

Steve wanted to help me pack everything that was job-related into the company car I'd been driving. I stood in the garage and hit the auto open trunk release on my Ford Taurus key fob. I had taken good care of this car even though it was technically not mine. Up popped the trunk, making the same noise it always had as it bounced off the hinges when reaching the fully ajar point. The trunk was neatly organized as always and had just a few boxes of marketing material in it, along with advertising pens neatly stacked in small cardboard boxes, waiting to be distributed when I made sales calls.

"Just throw everything in here and in the back seat," I instructed Steve. He looked doubtful about getting all the materials into such limited space, but he gamely began lifting and juggling.

A section of my garage was dedicated to my pharmaceutical company's product marketing materials. We had come a long way from storing drug samples in our garages from when I had first started all those years ago. It always amazed me that we had drugs literally stacked ceiling high in our home garages. Now was a different time, after drug law revisions, with much less stuff to store and account for. I was afraid to pick up anything heavy in fear something might happen to my baby. I pointed to all the boxes Steve needed to pack along with my computer, printer, and other miscellaneous work equipment.

The task was almost complete when, with a groan, Steve noticed something he hadn't figured on needing to pack.

"What should I do with these winter tires?" Steve asked. "There's no room left in the car." I was determined to clear any reminders of my job from my home and from my mind.

"Make room somehow. Stuff them wherever you can. I don't want my boss to have to come back for anything," I said.

After some rearranging, he managed to pack everything in the car. Afterward, I went inside and sent my boss an email telling him everything was ready for pickup. We made arrangements for him to come pick up the car and have me sign all the necessary paperwork to terminate my employment.

The next day, my boss, driven by his wife, pulled into my driveway. I stood in my garage as he approached me and the overfilled car. He walked toward me with a file folder in his hand. He knew I was angry. And why wouldn't I be? The conversation was short. I had lost all respect for him after how he treated me when I was pregnant with Jenny. I had no time for him then and certainly not now. After signing everything necessary, I stared at him as I handed him my keys. I wanted to say the most terrible things to him at that moment; however, I chose to stand and watch as he got in my company car. The back brake lights shone toward me as he put his foot on the brake while turning the ignition switch and putting the car in drive. I could see my winter tires through the back window along with boxes of literature and loose papers literally filling any empty space in the back seat. I wasn't keeping anything. Even down to the free pens. I reminisced for a moment about all the traveling I had done in that car. I spent my days driving, making and receiving phone calls, thinking about life, learning about life, eating, drinking coffee, and just doing my job, which I had enjoyed. It had been my second home.

The car inched to the end of the driveway and into the road, and slowly proceeded up the street and faded into the distance. I couldn't help but stand in the garage and think how this was one big chapter of my life closing, while another one was just beginning. I had made the right decision, although I was unsure what was to come. The spot where my car was always parked was now empty. I no longer had a car, no longer had a job, but knew in my heart the best was in front of me. I walked back to my garage toward the entry to the house, pushed the square white illuminated garage door opener attached to the wall, and watched as the garage door slowly closed as if it were the curtain coming down on the last act of a performance.

The weather was beginning to turn. I could hear the school buses coming through the neighborhood in the morning and afternoon. Another school year, another autumn. It had been almost a month since I had left work. I was isolated and a little lonely. Everyone was telling me that I should have put up a serious fight with my company. I didn't have the energy to fight. I was solely focused on having a healthy baby. I knew that if I was able to be lucky enough to become a mom, I would not return to work. Steve and I had talked about having a family and what it would look like prior to even trying.

We agreed that I would be a full-time mom. Although I never anticipated my career to be so promising or enjoyable, I began to waiver over staying home full time. Losing Jenny, however, centered me on what was important. Being a mom was all that mattered to me; therefore, climbing the corporate ladder fell off my radar. I had worked in some capacity since I was a young girl and now, not having a job, was leaving a large void within me. I didn't know what to do with myself or my time. I liked a full schedule. Busy was good. Here I was, not feeling well enough to do much and frightened to not do much of anything at all. I spent many days lying on my couch with Maude Lilly by my side. I talked with her as if she would somehow be able to talk back. I continued with my weekly doctor visits and tried hard to keep the positive messages cycling through my mind. I knew I needed to rest and care for myself, but some days proved difficult and depressing, and Steve saw that.

"I think we should buy a car," he said, reminding me that we were down to one car since turning in my company car a month ago.

"I don't think we should buy a car right now," I replied, shaking my head.

"I can't do anything or go anywhere while I follow my doctor's orders now anyway. Let's just wait and see what happens. Once I have the baby, we can figure out the car situation."

As the days came and went, the stress grew. Having so much time on my hands only gave me more time to worry. I had wanted a reduced job schedule that would allow me to combine rest and work. Forced out, I had nothing to take up my time and I grew restless. As I progressed further along in my pregnancy, I thought constantly of Jenny, and I kept worrying that the same thing might happen again. I tried hard to keep these thoughts at bay; however, when I didn't feel well or when there was little movement from my baby, the fear crept back in. I needed to be creative in finding something to occupy my mind.

I had always wanted to earn an MBA, and I decided to look into applying to graduate school for admission in the coming year. I researched different local programs and settled on applying to Syracuse University. This pursuit allowed me to focus on something positive. I applied and was accepted into the program for the spring of 2004. I had openly communicated with them that I was pregnant and was unsure what the outcome might be for me. The admissions staff assured me my acceptance would be honored when I was ready. I could take a few classes here and there, if need be, or a full academic load if that was the decision on my part. It was up to me. Having been accepted allowed me to look forward to going back to school at some point, and I found this exciting.

My parents and friends continued to be a great support system. My mom made the drive from Endicott every week to help with anything I needed and provide some much-needed moral support. Most importantly, she would take me out for an afternoon drive just to get me out of the house. I didn't want to go many places or do much of anything because I already did not feel well and was fearful of picking up a virus or anything that might harm my baby.

In my mind, I kept preventing myself from getting too excited about having a baby. It was that little speck of doubt. That's all it took to smother any sort of excitement or anticipation over what was yet to come. I could not endure another loss as I had with Jenny.

At each doctor's visit, I caught myself holding my breath walking into the office. It was as if I were bracing for something terrible. My heart was guarded, and how could it not be?

“Jenny, things are looking good. Keep resting,” Dr. Randolph said.

“I'm trying,” I said, my voice quivering.

These weekly visits became routine, but they were never without worry. That's why I was happy when, one week, my mom was with me. We spent the hour talking about old times and keeping it light while Dr. Randolph monitored the baby to make sure things were going well. It was the same thing every week. I would go to the office, sit in the cozy recliner while they applied sticky tape and numerous probes to my belly. Once the machine was turned on, a small, white paper printout slowly would appear as if it was a receipt coming out of a register. The paper would begin to gather on the carpeted floor in a small pile. Afterward, Dr. Randolph would come in and closely analyze the paper printout from start to finish looking for anything that might be of concern. He would reassure me, as would Lori, his nurse, always sending me off with a caring goodbye. I knew the only relief for me would come when I could finally hold my baby in my arms. I often found myself daydreaming about it being the end of February. I kept wishing the days away while enduring what seemed like the longest days ever.

Christmas 2003

Steve and I were relieved when I passed the six-month mark of my pregnancy in November. Despite being hesitant, I decided to have a pregnancy photo taken by my wedding photographer, Lisa. So many women I knew were having these beautiful photos taken so as to remember this special moment in time. I kept going back and forth about it and felt that if things went well, I might regret not having a pregnancy photo to cherish. I was so superstitious about it, that I made Lisa promise to keep the photos under wraps until the baby arrived and all was well.

In late fall, I heard the geese call from outside as they flew south. This time, I did not get up and go out front to see them off. I laid on the couch and prayed that this time things would be different upon their return. Thanksgiving had come and gone; we were fully into the holiday season. As the baby we wanted so desperately grew in my womb, I found it difficult to get a good night's sleep. But even though I was tired, I wanted to keep all the traditions we treasured and that I knew we would continue with our child in the years ahead.

It was mom to the rescue once again as I wondered if I dared disobey my doctor's ban on lifting and how I could muster the energy to deck the halls. Answering the telephone one frosty early

December morning, I was happy to recognize a cheerful voice.

"I'm coming up to help you decorate. Make sure you don't lift anything or do anything strenuous until I am there," Mom insisted on the other end of the phone.

Already past the six-month mark and still feeling unwell, I was frustrated. My body grew larger every week. I had never been able to shed the extra 15 pounds I had gained while pregnant with Jenny and now I was closing in on another 25. I really felt it when I would go up and down the stairs. Even simple exercise left me winded and struggling to catch my breath. I realized there would never be a "turning the corner" moment for my body as long as I was pregnant. Once I delivered the baby, I would get back to feeling like myself. I was sure of this.

When Mom arrived, we shared happy chatter as she unpacked the holiday trimmings and decorated the house. She lightened a sad time for me by creating a beautifully decorated home without making me feel guilty that I couldn't help more. I managed to put some ornaments on the tree, a sharp change from what I was used to doing for Christmas. By the time Mom left, everything looked festive, and Steve and I tried to maintain a sense of celebration.

As Christmas and baby Jenny's birthday drew closer, however, I felt a cloud of sadness come over me. I kept thinking back to the day I was preparing for the holidays by baking cookies for Steve's office party. I couldn't shake the memory of that one startling movement followed by stillness. I pictured the day she was born. Her angelic face, her tiny hands all wrapped in that soft blanket.

As I awoke on December 21, I felt emotionally heavy. I had woken in the night almost to the hour that Jenny was born. Perhaps it was a sign that she was okay. It had been a few months since I had dreamed of her being held by my grandmother Miriam, who had passed away in the mid-1990s. There they were, standing in a kitchen. My grandma beautifully dressed as she always was in a perfectly coordinated outfit of light purple, with her beehive hairstyle and her cat eyeglasses. As always, she had the most beautiful smile. In my dream, baby Jenny was dressed in a light pink, frilly dress with a matching frilly bonnet and white shoes. She looked happy and comfortable in my grandmother's arms. Both looked toward me as if they knew I was watching. My grandma was holding Jenny's little hand and waving hello to me. They looked so happy. When I woke up and realized it had been just a dream, I took it as a sign that they were together, happy and, most importantly, watching over me. That dream was a great comfort to me, and I revisited it often.

As was our custom, Steve and I, along with Maude Lilly, headed to Endicott to be with our families for the holidays. I was excited to get out of the house, to have a change of scenery, and to spend time with our loved ones. I wasn't in the mood to really do much of anything for the holiday as I was focused on trying to get to my pregnancy finish line and I was feeling physically uncomfortable. I worried that if I was around too many people, I would contract some sort of virus or illness that would threaten the well-being of my developing baby. The days seemed to be a tug of war in my mind throughout the entire month of December. I wanted to start to feel the excitement about having a baby; however, at the same time I was taken back through my memory of what had happened just prior to Christmas the year before. I was in a mental state of wanting to have that forward momentum but for some reason not being able to have any momentum at all. Therefore, we kept Christmas simple. We went to Steve's house to visit with his family and exchange gifts. I spent some time with my best friend Lisa, keeping it light and having our annual gift exchange just as we had every year since we were young girls. It was so great to have the support of my best friend. I know she was worried for me; we had known each other for 30 years and having a friend that long is a treasure. My mom made her traditional Christmas food of filet and lobster tail. In keeping with tradition, she placed her cookie platter on the table for dessert. All of our favorites are homemade by her year after year. The nut cups were always my top choice followed by the decorated sugar cookie and chocolate drop with vanilla frosting adorned with red and green sprinkles. Aside from the cookie platter, my mom would use the small, shiny, green Christmas tree-shaped cookie plate that had been my grandmother Miriam's. Each year, it would be full of chocolates from Victoria's. This had been a staple my entire life. My grandmother sold chocolates for extra money when my mom was a young girl growing up in Hazleton, Pennsylvania. At Christmastime, we always had Victoria's. To this day, a box from Victoria's is one of my most cherished gifts.

Because I was having so much difficulty being physically uncomfortable, I found it hard to really enjoy anything. Even Christmas. It was always a tradition for my mom and I to enjoy some shopping the day after Christmas. We would purchase some wrapping paper along with toys at a discount. This year, however, I had to tell my mom I wasn't up for it. She didn't think it was a good idea anyhow. I was looking forward to getting the holiday behind me as I was anticipating what was yet to come in the new year. A healthy baby.

We stopped by the cemetery with flowers and a candle to be lit for Jenny on our way back to Syracuse. The sun was shining down just as it had that day a little over a year ago when I said goodbye to her. I could see my breath as I bent down in front of the headstone that had recently been placed. As I looked at the shiny front of the stone and the little angel with just one date engraved December 21, 2002, I couldn't help but reflect on all that had happened in just over 365 days. I wondered what the next 365-plus days would bring. I said goodbye to her, walked back to the car with Steve, and headed north on Route 81.

We didn't have plans to celebrate the coming of the new year with friends, so it would be just the two of us in our own home.

"I'd like to have something nice to eat for New Year's Eve," Steve said as he looked at me lying on the couch.

I was having a hard time eating and tolerating food due to how large I had gotten from my pregnancy. It seemed as if everything I ate led to a stomachache or indigestion.

"What do you think you might want to eat?" I asked.

"I love prime rib. I'm thinking about making that for us. Would you eat that?"

"Yeah, I'll try," I said.

Steve always enjoyed cooking, so he headed out to shop for all the supplies to make a nice New Year's Eve dinner for us.

Dinner was nice; however, neither of us could manage to stay awake and ended up falling asleep before the arrival of 2004.

A New Year

I woke up with spit filling my mouth. I swallowed, then swallowed again. I jumped out of my bed and ran into the bathroom. I began vomiting.

"What's going on?" Steve asked, as he stood looking at me face down over the toilet.

"I'm so nauseous," I said before vomiting again.

I grabbed a washcloth, ran it under cold water and held it on my face for a moment before wiping my mouth with it. I looked in the mirror at my pale face and wondered what was going on.

"Can you go get me something to drink? Ginger ale, Gatorade, anything to keep my body hydrated," I said to Steve in a panic.

I sat on the edge of the tub, afraid to leave the bathroom in case I was going to vomit again.

"Here," Steve said, as he handed me a bottle of orange Gatorade.

I took a few small sips from the bottle and waited to see if there would be any sort of immediate reaction from my body. I started to feel some relief after fifteen minutes and felt as if the vomiting was starting to pass. I walked back to my side of the bed and sat on the edge for several minutes. I decided that I would go downstairs to the recliner and rest there for the remainder of the night.

"I don't think the prime rib agreed with me," I said to Steve, as he stood by the recliner looking at me.

"I am feeling much better now that I threw up."

My stomach seemed to be cramping a bit. I was getting worried that the vomiting might throw me into labor. I kept sipping the Gatorade as I sat in the recliner. I had made it this far and I did not want my baby coming early.

"I think I will be okay," I said to Steve, as I threw a blanket over myself. I closed my eyes and fell in and out of sleep.

The next day I woke up and felt better for the most part.

"I don't think I'll ever eat prime rib again," I said to Steve.

Just saying prime rib made me want to gag.

Over the next couple of days, I felt pain in my stomach. I didn't think I could wait for my weekly appointment, so I called the office. Dr. Randolph was on rounds, so his office instructed me to go to St. Joseph's Hospital where they had a triage unit so he could check on me there. Once I arrived, they immediately made me lie down in bed and proceeded to monitor the baby. I was having contractions. I had told them about my vomiting a few days prior. I couldn't help but wonder why everything connected to my delivering a healthy baby was so challenging.

"I am having a difficult time getting the cannula into a vein," the nurse said as she held my right hand and poked me again.

I didn't realize I was so dehydrated. I had tried hard to drink large amounts of water since my vomiting incident. I noticed the nurse was still having difficulty finding a vein. I began to sweat from the pain she was causing by trying time and time again to insert the needle. Abandoning my usual patience, I just wanted the pain to stop.

"Can you find someone else to try?" I blurted out, without giving much thought to her feelings.

The more she tried to establish the IV, the more painful it became.

"Please get someone else to do this," I begged.

Steve stood in the corner where the curtain was drawn on the lower right side of my bed. I could tell he was getting queasy watching the nurse trying to establish an IV. His phone rang and he excused himself into the hall.

A few minutes later another nurse came in and was able to get the needle inserted on the first try. I felt great relief, although my hand was sore and throbbing. She immediately started a fluid drip to see if it might help slow the contractions. The nurse then took me for a sonogram.

She informed me that they needed to take a look at the baby and make sure everything was good. They also wanted to rule out any gallbladder issues that might have contributed to the vomiting. After that, she wheeled me back to the triage unit. Meanwhile, Steve had come back in from his call. Unsure if they could get the contractions to stop with the IV fluids and other meds they were administering, I was beginning to worry about what was to come.

As the contractions continued, Dr. Randolph came in to speak with Steve and me. He had taken a look at the sonogram that had been done along with the fetal monitoring of the baby. He informed us that it looked as though I was indeed having continuous contractions. He felt it was important to try to stop labor. The nurse was on her way to give me medicine and additional intravenous fluids to try to accomplish this. Worst-case scenario was that the baby would come under some sort of duress, and he would have to deliver the baby sooner rather than later.

He sensed my immediate concern and spoke in a calm manner that it was early for the baby's arrival; however, they could give me some medicine to try to speed up the baby's lung development. The doctor encouraged me not to worry or panic as it wasn't good for the baby, and he felt that everything would be just fine. He wanted to let me know ahead of time in the event it became an emergency situation so that I didn't panic. From what he could see from the testing, it looked like I had some bile backup in my gallbladder, and this may be why I had experienced stomach pain and vomiting. He assured me that if they could get the contractions under control, I would be okay. He needed to get back to seeing other patients, so he said if I needed anything to tell the nurses and they would contact him.

"How long is this going to take?" Steve asked as he pointed to the face of his watch. His question stung as much as the many attempts the first nurse had made inserting the cannula. I glared at my husband, angry at what I thought was his insensitivity.

"How long is this going to take, Steve?" I snapped. "I really have no idea!"

"Do you want me to call your mom?" Steve asked.

"No. Not until we know what is going on."

I was feeling all kinds of emotions. One thing was for sure, I was scared, and Steve and I were not handling the stress of the situation very well.

The meds began to work, and things were looking up. The medical team continued to observe me for most of the day and, after additional testing of both me and the baby, they released me and instructed me to go home and just rest.

My mom came up to pack away all the Christmas decorations. As I lay on the couch watching her take things down, I couldn't help but think ahead to next Christmas. Would I finally be able to decorate with a baby in tow? As I pondered that thought, I immediately brought myself right back to the current day. I was afraid to look ahead like that.

I continued to see Dr. Randolph on a weekly basis, and he had technicians perform a weekly stress test on the baby to make sure all was well. Everyone in the office was pulling for us. My friends and family continued to support me. Some days, a simple phone call was just what I needed to keep my mind steady and my mood upbeat.

By mid-January, I was in the homestretch.

My mom called to urge me to think about getting ready for the baby's arrival. She wanted me to think about going shopping for some basic baby items. She suggested coming to pick me up and thought it might be a nice idea to bring me down to her and my dad's house for a few days. She felt the change of scenery would do me good and wanted to take me to a local baby furniture shop to look at cribs and changing tables. I was having a difficult time trying to bring myself to think about buying anything for the baby. I knew I would need the basics to bring the baby home. What a different experience this was compared to most. I never really thought that this would be my experience. I guess deep down inside I felt worried about buying anything as I wasn't sure what the outcome would be. This was the reality for me. And it scared me.

My mom picked me up and brought me down to her and my dad's house for a few days as she had suggested. It was nice to get out of my house and have a change of scenery. Nice to spend time with my parents and talking about all kinds of things. Except for one. Having a baby. We avoided it for the most part. My mom and I ventured out late one morning to the baby furniture store. We were greeted by a nice saleswoman who was eager to help me find just the right crib and changing table. She had no idea how uncomfortable it was for me to be there. Something that should have been full of fun and excitement was overshadowed by uncertainty. I wasn't sure what I wanted or what I was looking for. I found the entire experience stressful and unenjoyable. I told my mom I wasn't sure if there was anything that really spoke to me, so we left without buying anything.

My mom and I had agreed that there would be no baby shower until after the baby arrived. After some trepidation, I did make the decision that I would need to go ahead and pick out a crib and changing table along with bedding before the baby's arrival. I also committed to buying a few basic things that were needed for when I brought the baby home. Steve and my parents convinced me to register at Babies R Us. We had people asking us what they could buy for us when the baby arrived, so we decided the best way to handle this was to create a registry.

On a weekend in January, Steve and I headed to the Babies R Us by the Carousel Mall. I handed Steve the scanner as we walked around aimlessly in the huge warehouse store. We decided to tackle the most important things first. The cribs and changing tables were located in the rear of the store. We then tackled the bedding. Since we didn't know the sex of the baby, we decided on a cute and simple primary-colored gingham crib set. Perfect for either a boy or a girl. As I walked around the store, I thought about how I had longed to have the whole experience of a big shower before the arrival of the baby. In my heart I wanted the experience of readying a nursery with everything organized and lovingly placed. Being able to bring my newborn home to a beautiful set-up nursery, as most new mothers do, was something that I had really hoped for. But I couldn't bring myself to do it. Maybe it was illogical, but I remained superstitious about taking any kind of step like that. The agreement was that I would have the room painted a pale yellow and that was all that would be done. No crib, no changing table, no bedding. Nothing until the baby arrived. My mom and dad agreed that when we all knew that the delivery went well and all was good, they would shop for the basics from my registry. I had shared with them the crib and changing table I picked out. My dad agreed since he was so handy, they would go get everything and my dad would assemble it all prior to our homecoming.

As I had so many times in my life, I gave thanks for my parents and their constant support. I was happy that we had firmed up many of the nursery details and that plans were firming up for a post-baby shower.

My gratitude extended to Dr. Randolph and his staff, who had skillfully extended my pregnancy and allowed the baby to continue to develop. Although some women relish the enforced slow-down of the final trimester, I was in too much discomfort to enjoy it. By late January I could barely stand the pain from my gallbladder issues. I asked the doctor when I would get some relief.

“I don’t think you're going to get any relief until the baby is delivered,” Dr. Randolph said, as I sat on the examining table holding my stomach.

“The pain comes and goes,” I said, “but at times it is unbearable. I’ve adjusted my diet and followed all your suggestions,” I said in frustration. Dr. Randolph was sympathetic, but he had to adhere to protocols.

“I need you to try and hold on until the baby is at week 37,” he said. “That's the earliest I would be able to deliver the baby.”

February 2004

I celebrated my thirty-second birthday on February 1. Dr. Randolph's office had called and scheduled an induction for February 6, the morning of week 37. Just five more days. Finally, I could see the finish line and the prize of a healthy baby.

Steve and I had openly shared our concerns and our hopes. After we announced our due date, we had tons of calls from friends and family wishing us well. So many people were thinking of us and praying for a healthy baby that it added to our peace of mind and our sense of gratitude. Although the six days seemed to go by in slow motion, inevitably, it was D-Day.

I stood in the shower with the warm water washing over me. It was 4:30 a.m. My baby bump made it difficult to get comfortable in bed, and my racing thoughts warded off sleep. I hadn't slept more than a half hour at a time all night. As I relaxed beneath the spray of the shower, I was daydreaming about the long, challenging journey that had brought me to this point. Breathing in the steam and daring to smile for the first time in weeks, I thought: Today, I will finally meet my baby.

I threw on a celery green velvet sweatsuit, put my hair up in a high bun, grabbed my packed bag and told Maude Lilly I would see her soon.

It was a cold and icy morning as Steve and I drove slowly along Onondaga Parkway in the Jeep. There was so much ice on the road that a few cars had spun out and were sitting on the shoulder with their hazard lights flashing. I kept telling Steve to drive slowly. Driving conditions were making me nervous and the weather forecast was calling for a whole day of freezing rain. I began to worry that my parents wouldn't be able to make the drive to arrive at the hospital in time for the delivery. Steve was also concerned his parents wouldn't make it. Being present for the birth of their grandchild was important to all of them.

We arrived and the automatic door opened. Once again, the hospital aroma overwhelmed me. My heart was beating fast as I took a few deep breaths. The team in labor and delivery was waiting for me. They put a slim white identification bracelet on me just as they had when I delivered Jenny. I was directed to a room that was much nicer than the one I had been given when Jenny was born. The room actually had a window, and I could see it was already getting light outside. I changed into my hospital gown, and they readied me to be induced. Dr. Randolph went over the induction process again and said maybe by early afternoon the baby would arrive.

All the medical staff went on to care for others, and it was just Steve and I as we waited for our parents' arrival.

I was visited by Mary, the nurse who had cared for me when I delivered Jenny. She had seen my name on the incoming patient list and decided to come and wish me well. She looked the same. Layered mid-length, dark brown hair, kindness radiating from her deep brown eyes, and a warm smile lighting up the room. I could sense her excitement for me. We had come full circle.

By late morning my parents had arrived, followed by Steve's parents. I was having some contractions, but progress was not as rapid as expected. Dr. Randolph broke my water and was hopeful the baby would arrive by mid-afternoon. But, I learned, babies have their own timetables.

Late morning turned into late afternoon and still not even close to having a baby. As the contractions increased, the baby did not like it. The baby's heartbeat would begin to drop on the fetal monitor each time. I began to grow anxious. Soon, the contractions became intense, and the baby was struggling. When he saw the baby's distress, Dr. Randolph decided it would be best to deliver the baby via C-section, and I was quickly wheeled into the operating room.

Before I knew it, I was prepped with a wide white sheet-curtain placed just above my waist. The anesthesiologist kept asking if I was okay and if I could feel anything. The only thing I could feel was the beat of my heart in my hands as each arm lay stretched straight out to each side.

"Just a few more minutes and you can grab her husband," I heard Dr. Randolph say to the nurse.

As I waited for Steve to get the clear to come in, no one said much of anything as everyone seemed to be working diligently. I looked up at the ceiling of the operating room; the cluster of shiny silver bright lights blinded me. I turned my head to the right and rested on my right ear. As I lay there looking to the right, I could see Dr. Randolph's feet as he was working on delivering the baby. I noticed that he had his regular shoes on. No surgical covers or anything. It made me think this was indeed an unexpected quick delivery. Instead of concentrating on what was going on, I stared at his shoes. They looked to be some sort of low ankle hiking boot. They were dark green with thick black soles with lots of traction grooves in the soles. Most notable was the amount of mud that encased them. I wondered where he had just been in those shoes. Was he hiking in the woods or just going from home to office to hospital in the messy winter conditions of Central New York? As I pondered this, Dr. Randolph started to talk to me about what he was doing. Steve came and sat by my side as the anesthesiologist was just above my head.

Years after Steve and I blithely decided to start our family, months from the irreconcilable loss of

Jenny, weeks of struggle as my body seemed to take the hardest possible journey through pregnancy, and days of waiting for this event all converged at one magnificent moment. At 5:07 p.m. our baby was born.

"It's a boy!" Dr. Randolph exclaimed, as the nurse held the most precious baby in the world close to my face so I could meet him for the first time. Every worry, struggle, fear, and apprehension fled, and I was deliriously happy.

The nurses tended to my baby boy. He weighed six pounds, ten ounces and was nineteen inches long. They noticed he had excess fluid in his lungs. I felt a slight return of worry when Dr. Randolph said they were going to send him to the NICU. But I could tell he was not concerned, and he told me that this was standard procedure.

"We will need to know what you are going to name him," the nurse said.

We weren't sure exactly what name to give him. We had come with a piece of paper which we had been keeping at home where we continually added both boys' and girls' names as the weeks and months passed. We had accumulated quite a list. We were really into the origin and meanings of the names we were considering. We also felt that we needed to meet our baby prior to actually giving him or her a name.

I felt woozy as they wheeled me to the recovery area. They had propped up the hospital bed so I could sit up. I couldn't believe how much better I was feeling physically already. The pediatrician came in and said our baby would have a short stay in the NICU until they could clear some of the fluid out of his lungs. Otherwise, he looked fantastic. I was relieved but was hoping to be able to hold him soon.

Dr. Randolph tried to put my mind at ease. "Jenny, it should only be about two to three hours. Please think about his name," he said.

After a few hours, the nurse brought our baby and handed him to me. Finally, I could hold my son. We were wheeled into a private room in the post-labor and delivery area. The nurses kept commenting on how they had never seen a new mom look so good. They had no idea. I felt like a million bucks. Even though I had just had a C-section, I wanted to jump up and down with joy. Steve and I took out our list and decided that we would name our baby Ethan. It was Hebrew in origin and most often meant strong. It was perfect for this child who had already demonstrated his strength and given some to his parents as well.

The nurse wheeled in a bassinet with Ethan's name on it and set it right next to my bed. The joy I felt was indescribable.

The pediatrician came in and said Ethan looked to have jaundice and that sometimes this can happen. I noticed the yellowing of his skin and wondered what it meant. The pediatrician said it was nothing to be concerned about and they would put him under some special lights if need be.

I was up walking the halls and proudly pushing Ethan around the maternity wing in his bassinet. I couldn't believe he was finally here, that he was healthy and beautiful, and that I felt restored to wellness.

The next morning, Dr. Randolph came to see how I was. I could sense his relief just by the tone of his voice. I was so grateful for him and the care he gave me. Lori from his office even called to say congratulations and how happy she was for us.

Mary tended to me when she was on shift, along with many other wonderful nurses. They helped me get comfortable breastfeeding, changing diapers, bathing Ethan, and soothing him. The time flew by until it was time for our little family to go home.

I sat in the wheelchair while Mary placed the car seat with Ethan in it on my lap. She gave me a big hug and wished us well. I choked up and found it hard to say thank you. She had no idea how much she made me feel loved and cared for. A nice woman came and wheeled us onto the elevator.

As the aide took us carefully down to the exit, I couldn't help but think back to the last time I was on this elevator. That time, I was alone. That time, I received a blessing. That time, I had faith that one day I would experience this exact moment, a moment of leaving St. Joseph's Hospital with a baby in my arms. I took a deep breath. The doors of the hospital entrance parted, and I could see Steve waiting out front with the car. Seeing Steve, I felt gratitude swell my heart again because this time, I was meeting him with our baby, and I was overwhelmed with gratitude.

"Can we stop at Heid's and grab a few hot dogs and cheese fries?" I asked Steve. After months of queasiness, I had a voracious appetite.

Steve looked surprised, then laughed. "Of course, we can."

It was a beautiful sunny day as we drove from the city along Onondaga Lake Parkway to Heid's.

While Steve ran in to grab the food, I couldn't see Ethan's face because the car seat was facing backward. He was quiet, and I wanted to make sure he was okay. I quickly got out of the car and opened the passenger side back door to check on him. I was relieved to see he was sleeping soundly and looked cozy all bundled up and nestled in the car seat.

Steve got into the driver's side, handed me the food and, as he put the car in reverse to get back on the road, I quickly opened the square styrofoam container and dived into the cheese fries. I munched and we talked about what a great day this was all the way home.

Maude Lilly jumped with joy at our arrival. We placed the car seat down in the living room so she could meet her new baby brother. Her tail wagged with joy as she tried to sneak a kiss in on him. The sun was shining through our back door slider window, so we placed Ethan at the sliding door to get some sun exposure, as the pediatrician had suggested. He was content, although still a glowy yellow.

My parents had been waiting for us to get settled before heading back to Endicott, so Steve and I could have some time to ourselves. Steve was taking a few days off of work and then my mom would come up to help me. Before they left, I went upstairs to see the nursery. I could see all the hard work my dad had put in assembling everything. Finally, I had a nursery, and it was just as I had imagined. I was grateful.

I burst into tears as I came back down the stairs and saw Ethan in the baby carrier. Tears of joy at the sight of my beautiful son. I was emotionally overwhelmed from this long journey to motherhood and at the same time still mourning the loss of my daughter. The collision of two distinctly separate feelings and experiences at once.

The early days of being a new mom were a whirlwind of activity as Steve and I made the adjustments every set of first-time parents must make. The recovery from a C-section and the regular trips to the lab for the bilirubin tests for jaundice were challenging. Despite following the pediatrician's instructions, Ethan's levels were still high. But, we were coping, and we were happy.

When I looked at Ethan, I couldn't help but think about baby Jenny. Even though she was so tiny and he was fully developed, the resemblance in their faces was striking. This beautiful boy was my reminder of the deep gratitude I felt for this journey. Every week, every day, Ethan was changing and growing, and each stage of his development was a gift of joy.

I recall a special morning when I could see Ethan as I loaded the dishwasher. He was busy figuring out how his Jumperoo worked. I had placed it between the kitchen and the dining room. He was happy to try to stand on his own with the support of the metal spring system as he bounced about. The more he bounced, the more he giggled. I loved hearing that giggle of his, full of pure joy. Winter had finally passed. I had opened the windows a crack first thing in the morning to let in some fresh air. I was looking forward to the arrival of spring so we could take long walks in the stroller with Maude Lilly by our side.

As I contemplated that pleasant activity, I stopped what I was doing and just listened. I could faintly hear the geese in the distance. I picked Ethan up and out of the Jumperoo and headed to the front door, checking to see if geese were actually around. Loud and louder they honked, as they flew in giant flocks over us and I stood with Ethan on the front porch. Looking up it felt so celebratory, so much a part of the hope I had held in my heart years ago. The geese were returning north, and there I was waiting for them, standing on my front porch with my baby.

The days and months passed quickly. I enjoyed being a new mom and enjoyed every moment with Ethan. I held him endlessly. He was an easy baby. Content and happy. The only difficulty I had was getting him to sleep. He didn't like to sleep. My mom–and many others–tried to give me advice as to why he wouldn't sleep. Perhaps it was because I was busy holding him all the time, so he didn't know how to soothe himself. Other theories were put forth, but I dismissed all the advice and did what I wanted to. If I wanted to hold Ethan and rock him to sleep or carry him in the BabyBjörn even when I vacuumed, that's what I was going to do. I wanted to be close to him every chance I had. I knew that he would grow and change quickly, and I didn't want to miss any of it. I was going to handle motherhood on my terms.

I had not forgotten, however, that I had made a plan to embark on a path of higher education. I started graduate school in early May and was enjoying it for the intellectual stimulation and socialization it provided. Sometimes, though, I wondered what I had gotten myself into. I was determined to strike a comfortable balance between motherhood and school. Still, there was never any question about what, or who, came first. It was always Ethan.

We met all the typical milestones. Ethan's first Valentine's Day, Easter, summer, fall and Christmas. I had looked forward to his first Halloween in the fall and splurged on an "Alley Cat" Halloween costume. Since we were on a budget, I felt guilty spending the $65 on a costume he would only wear once. I couldn't help myself though and had professional pictures taken in it for longevity. I wanted to give him the best of everything. To this day, the "Alley Cat" costume ranks as one of my top favorites for Halloween picks of all time.

Before I knew it, we were celebrating Ethan's first birthday. I wasn't sure what I was going to do for his birthday, but I knew I wanted it to be special. After some thought, I decided on a small family party with the grandparents, close friends, and a few neighbors. I settled on a Winnie-The-Pooh theme. I wanted to make the cake from scratch and decorate it to the best of my ability. I also decided that I would make Ethan a small round cake for himself to dive into and eat however he wanted. I'll never forget how he picked up that cake with his hands and devoured it.

After Ethan turned one in February. Steve and I decided that we were ready to try to have another baby. The joy Ethan had given us was overwhelming, and we agreed the more children, the better. I wasn't hesitant about having more children, but I was hesitant about going through another pregnancy to get there. Knowing how my body reacted to pregnancy, I actually dreaded it. I still felt fearful deep down inside about having another loss, but I had gained some confidence with the birth of Ethan. I talked it over with Dr. Randolph, and he felt good about the idea. I wondered about school. I was knee-deep in classes and it was tough. I was committed to getting my degree but knew taking a leave from coursework was necessary.

The heat of early summer had arrived. I lay on the carpet in Ethan's bedroom stacking blocks with him as we did most mornings. The switch had been flipped. I felt nauseous and tired. I was having difficulty. I wondered why I was doing this to myself again. I had Ethan. I had pondered this decision to have another child for some time. Long talks with my mom about her being an only child had helped me in my thoughts about going forward to have another child. We often talked about how she wished she had a sibling. Her mom, my grandmother Miriam, almost died in childbirth, so she was unable to have any additional children. We talked about how I felt about having an only child and I knew I wanted Ethan to have a sibling.

I met all the pregnancy milestones and, even though this pregnancy seemed like a carbon copy of Ethan's, I was navigating through the months with a sense of assurance, knowing that I had already traveled this route successfully. I had a few gallbladder issues and scares along the way, but for the most part, it was the same long journey. Dr. Randolph, as always, kept a close eye on me. We had the success of Ethan behind us, so we were feeling good about making it to the finish line.

I was grateful for my mom who would make the drive up from Endwell once a week to take Ethan to the Great Northern Mall, so I could just rest. Ethan loved the time with his grandma and vice versa. He was obsessed with Elmo at the time, so when they passed by Mrs. Field's cookies and he spotted a plastic Elmo cookie bucket, my mom was happy to stop and have him pick the cookies he wanted to fill it up. I still remember his excitement carrying his bright red Elmo cookie bucket by the handle upon their return home. The once-a-week trip to the mall always produced something-Elmo being brought home with a big smile. It was good for me to rest and good for Ethan to be able to get out of the house. Sometimes, my mom would stay overnight if I needed a solid night's sleep. She would tend to Ethan in the night which I know she loved. That one night a week of undisturbed sleep did me wonders. I had decided to push the pause button on graduate school and knew I would dive back in when the time was right. I felt so much the same, that I was convinced I would be having another boy. Steve and I both decided that we would again not learn the sex of the baby. In my heart, however, I was expecting a boy.

I began to think about how I would feel not having a baby girl and how it might affect me, if at all. I spoke openly with my mom about it. Although I had tried to make peace with the loss of baby Jenny, I knew it would continue to be difficult for me. Time would most likely make the hurt a little less, but that void I felt in my heart would remain. Even though I had a deep belief that everything happens for a reason, it was still something I was trying to come to terms with. I began to realize, in trying to process my thoughts and emotions, that I almost feared having a little girl in some strange way. If I ended up having a girl, I did not want to feel like I was replacing Jenny or would forget her memory. These thoughts were difficult for me to make sense of. I would always come back to my faith. I knew God would give me what he wanted me to have. If I was meant to have a girl, I would be given a girl, and if I was meant to have a boy, I would be given a boy. I had faith in that. I found peace in that.

Dr. Randolph had told me we would deliver by Cesarean section again, and one day, I came home from the grocery store to a message on my answering machine.

"Hi, this is Dr. Randolph's office calling to schedule you for your C-section. Dr. Randolph would like to deliver your baby on February 6, the morning of the 37th week. Please call us to confirm this message."

I laughed out loud. Are they crazy, I thought? That is Ethan's birthday. I picked up the phone and called the office. The staff had no idea that Ethan had been delivered exactly two years prior on February 6. I told the surgery scheduler I thought they were playing a joke on me. We laughed. She said she would check with Dr. Randolph about another delivery date.

The nurse called me back and said she had spoken with Dr. Randolph, and he wanted to know if I could hold on another week and that he would like to deliver the baby on Valentine's Day.

"Perfect!" I replied.

I was surprised at the reaction some people had to having a baby on Valentine's Day. They either loved the idea or disliked it. I thought it was great and that was all that mattered.

We arrived at the hospital early on Valentine's Day. This was a completely different experience than the one with Ethan. We went in knowing that I was going to have a C-section. For the most part, I knew what to expect. Dr. Randolph's office forgot to let me know that the C-section had been pushed out to 8:45 a.m. I showed up two hours earlier than

I should have. Dr. Randolph was apologetic, telling me there had been a scheduling mix up. It wasn't a big deal to me. I would patiently wait. I called my parents, who were taking care of Ethan, and told them not to rush to the hospital. Steve called his parents and told them not to rush either. I was really excited and much less nervous than I had been two years before.

My mom and dad showed up with Ethan several hours later. It was exciting to see my little guy, knowing in just a few hours he would be a big brother. I had wanted that so much for him.

Steve was dressed in his scrubs and was told to wait outside the delivery room until they were ready for him. This time the delivery was not rushed as it had been with Ethan. It was a more relaxed environment, which I appreciated. I was wheeled into the operating room and told to move from the gurney onto the operating table. I noticed so much more this time around than when Ethan was delivered. It was a city of stainless steel. The anesthesiologist was there along with Dr. Randolph, another assisting physician, and the nursing staff. This time things went slowly.

"Ouch!" I said as the needle went in my back.

"Keep your head down and please stay very still," the doctor said.

I lay back on the table with my arms out as the sheet-screen was put up just above my waist. I felt nervous as I had my wits about myself this time and was fully aware of what was going on. The anesthesiologist kept reassuring me. Steve came in as they were starting. Nothing ever hurt me, but the pressure I felt was overwhelming. Dr. Randolph seemed to be having a hard time getting the baby out. The assisting physician was pushing on my belly while Dr. Randolph was gently pulling. At 9:34 a.m., my little Valentine Erich was born. He weighed seven pounds, seven and a half ounces and was twenty inches long. The nurses and pediatrician took care of him, as the doctors took care of me. A few minutes later the sheet above my waist came down and the nurse propped my bed up. The nurse came over and handed me Erich, who was tightly wrapped in a blanket. Holding my newborn son as they wheeled me out to recovery was an amazing moment.

I was in recovery when my parents brought Ethan in to meet his new baby brother. The look of amazement on his face was something I would never forget. It was official, he was indeed a big brother, and he would be a great one. That much I knew.

Erich was a bit bruised on his face from the delivery. The nurses said they had never seen a C-section baby come out bruised like that. It must have been the pushing and pulling to get him out. By all other accounts, he was healthy and that was all that mattered.

I was hurting from the C-section. It was much more painful than what I remembered from Ethan's birth. The nurse had me move from the bed to the chair by late evening. She told me the importance of moving after a C-section. This was a different recovery experience for me. I was walking laps after Ethan's delivery and now I struggled to just move my body. The pain I felt was intense. Erich was content. The nurses said he had to be one of the calmest, happiest newborns they had seen.

Mary was my nurse again, and I felt fortunate to have her tend to Erich and me. She asked if she could bring Erich to the newborn class for expecting parents. She brought him back and said he didn't even cry when he had his sponge bath. She laughed and informed the attending parents, your baby will not be this calm.

"You're one lucky mom," she said, giving me a hug. I never doubted her for a moment.

A Family of Four

I realized every day how lucky I was to have the boys. When I thought back to how I envisioned becoming a mother, this was not the journey I had imagined. Being the planner I had always been, I thought I had it all worked out. I would have my first child at or around 30 and take it from there, never thinking or imagining the lesson I would learn along the way. As I watched Ethan dote over his baby brother, I realized that for all the planning you can do in life, there really is no planning because you never know what lies around the corner. I was happy to have ended up lucky at the end of the day.

As all four of us settled in as a family, along with Maude Lilly who was never far, we enjoyed all the moments life presented to us. Steve was busy providing for us, while I nurtured the boys at home and took care of the house, finances and life in general. As the older brother, Ethan was my little helper and loved his baby brother. That special bond they shared made my heart full: Ethan was always wanting to hold his little brother or help in any way. A caring, proud, big brother as I positioned his arms, so he could safely hold him a few times a day. We had fun trying to get a smile or coo out of Erich while making silly faces and noises. Ethan always ended up laughing the most watching me create a silly face or make strange sounds. Erich would then smile or coo listening to his brother's sweet laugh.

Maude Lilly also enjoyed having another little one in the house to watch over. I had always thought she would have been a good beagle mom and a part of me was sad that I had never let her have any puppies. She seemed happy watching over the boys and when Erich would cry due to hunger or discomfort of some sorts, she would come immediately to make sure he was indeed okay. And when I couldn't find her during Ethan's nap, I would find her happily content sleeping in front of his crib. When I would see the boys interacting, my hope for these two little boys was that they would always remain close. They would always love each other, support each other, regardless of what life presented them. In these moments, that's what I silently prayed for.

After days of being home with family, I dressed, put on makeup and drove to Dr. Randolph's office for a six-week, post-delivery follow-up appointment. My mom had come up to watch the boys so that I didn't have to take them along. As I drove, I realized Erich was already a month-and-a-half old, and Ethan seemed to be growing and learning every day. Life was great. We had our routine and I was still basking in the glow of motherhood all over again.

Dr. Randolph greeted me with a big handshake and smile as he always did. I felt as if he was congratulating me all over again and, really, congratulating himself as well. I could sense his relief that once again we had made it to the finish line. I told Dr. Randolph it wouldn't have been possible without his care and his insistence that I adhere to his instructions.

After examining me and asking about the boys, the doctor initiated a frank conversation about whether I saw myself having more children. At 34 years old and knowing that Steve and I would want to wait a few years before trying to get pregnant again, I was trying to be realistic. I knew in my heart I was not willing to push the envelope.

I explained to Dr. Randolph that I had always hoped to have a large family. How I never envisioned the difficulty in becoming a mother that I would encounter or even the quick passage of years while enjoying my career which led me to starting a family later than I thought I would. But, here I was, almost in my mid-thirties and having encountered the loss of Jenny and the blessing of Ethan and Erich.

"There is a part of me that wants so much to be able to have more children. However, the realist side of me knows that this journey has been anything but smooth, and now that I have Ethan and Erich, there is this deep intuition that I should move on and be grateful for coming this far. To not push the envelope. To not test my luck," I explained to Dr. Randolph.

"It certainly has been very stressful, Jenny. Pregnancy has not only been hard on you physically, but emotionally. You're in your mid-thirties and I am unsure how your body will handle another pregnancy. It could go either way. In my professional opinion, you should think long and hard about having another baby. In the end, though, this is ultimately your decision," Dr. Randolph said with a serious look on his face.

I knew what Dr. Randolph truly thought without him even having to say it: That I should be grateful for getting to this point. He had no idea my mom had told me that when he delivered Erich and came out of the operating room to tell them all was well, the relief on his face and in his voice was apparent. I believe he felt immense stress and pressure, too.

I left Dr. Randolph's office that day knowing that my family was complete. I felt it was the right decision based on the doctor's advice and what my gut was telling me, and I was grateful to him for his extraordinary care throughout all my pregnancies. Most importantly, I left that office with deep joy for the two beautiful boys who, in years to come, would enrich my life to a greater degree than I could ever have imagined.

The months passed quickly as I learned to balance the needs of two children. When Erich napped, that was time for Ethan and me, and vice versa. Laundry piled up, the house was not nearly as organized or clean as it once had been. Taking each day as it came, enjoying life with my two boys was full of happiness. I returned to graduate school in summer. My parents pitched in when they could to help me when I had a big exam or project due. I was in the homestretch of completing my degree, so I continued to press forward. I also hired a college student, Jenna, who came twice a week to watch the boys while I attended class or went to the library to complete work. I was a juggler, keeping many balls in the air, and often feeling exhausted. But it was all worth it.

Erich was growing quickly. We celebrated holidays, Easter, Mother's Day and Memorial Day, and went about life. I watched as Erich became more alert and how Ethan and Erich bonded as brothers. Ethan tended to his little brother's needs. He always brought him little toys, and as Erich started to try and roll over on his little play mat, Ethan was right there alongside him, trying to teach him and encourage him. And when the moment came that he did finally roll over, Ethan was a proud big brother. When Erich became big enough to safely navigate his baby walker, Ethan was right there encouraging him to chase him. Ethan giggled with excitement while Erich squealed in delight. My heart was full. I was a mom to two terrific little boys and, always in my heart, to a tiny girl at rest in that cemetery in Johnson City who came to me in dreams. I often thought what a joy she would have been and how she might have been a big sister to the boys. It just wasn't meant to be. This was the reality; this was the way our lives were meant to be.

I continued to take courses and graduated with my MBA in June of 2007. I had met my academic goals and felt a strong sense of accomplishment. Ethan was three years old and Erich one. The boys and I kept busy with outings to the park, zoo, mall, and down to the Binghamton area. Panera was our go-to early in the morning, followed by a grocery adventure through Wegmans to see their train, which was suspended from the ceiling. Lots of simple moments, such as a picnic in the backyard and "Thomas the Train" videos, which both boys enjoyed. Steve traveled and worked hard making sure we had what we needed as a family. It was important for us to be able to make ends meet while I had the privilege of staying home to raise the boys.

The boys were good travelers, and they relished the frequent trips we made to visit my mom and dad. My parents had quite the collection of toys at their house and the boys always looked forward to playing with different things. One of the boys' favorites was the green turtle sandbox. Both looked forward to spending hours in it with all their little trucks and sand toys. My mom had it placed on her covered back porch to keep it out of the sun and away from any animals wanting to use it as a litter box. It was large enough for both of them to sit barefoot and feel the sand between their toes while scooping up the sand with their favorite plastic dump trucks. They also looked forward to adventures through the woods by my parents' house looking for little bugs or leaf treasures. When they were ready for some food, a trip for pizza, chicken tenders, and french fries at a local bar-and-restaurant ensued. The big deal at the restaurant was that the boys helped themselves to whatever they wanted to drink out of the sliding glass drink cooler. Making the decision about which drink to choose was always tough. Typically, a soda of some flavor as a treat was the final pick.

And then there was my dad's garden. The boys were in awe of what he would be growing and how they were able to just pick tomatoes, cucumbers, or the beans growing vertically on the beanpole my dad had made out of small pieces of wood and string. They loved being able to eat everything immediately, fresh and delicious from nature. In the fall, there were trips to the pumpkin farm to pick a special pumpkin and see all the animals. If the ice cream stand was still open, a quick stop there for a treat. And on one occasion, my dad took Ethan to the horse farm one morning to see the horses get their new shoes. This was during Ethan's love-of-horses phase where he carried around a Breyer Appaloosa horse named Speckle Butt. The horse phase required weekly trips to Target to see if any new Breyer horses had been put on the shelf that he didn't already have. And in the evening or when it rained, it was all about Play-Doh. My mom had everything organized in a small plastic bin filled with all kinds of Play-Doh tools and cutouts. One of the boys' favorites was a small tube they stuffed with the color of their choice and when pushed through, it made silly hair on the face on one side of the plastic tube. They would try to carry the plastic bin out by themselves, but they always yielded to allow us to help in the end.

No trip to be with family was ever complete until we made a stop at the cemetery to visit Jenny. In the trunk, I always carried a bouquet of seasonal flowers and a candle to be lit to remind us of the light our baby girl had brought into the world. At Christmastime, I made and placed a fresh fir wreath adorned with a big handmade bow on Jenny's headstone. These traditions began immediately after her burial, and I will never allow the Christmas holiday or Jenny's birthday to pass without honoring her with a visit and a prayer. When the boys were still young, I knew they would not be able to fully understand why their mommy would stop at this place and do these things. At some point, I realized, the day would come when they would be curious, and they would ask me why we were stopping here. When that time came, I would tell them in terms they could understand.

As days became months and months became years, we made our left turn into the cemetery as we always had and proceeded up and around the outer perimeter. The boys were older on this visit: Ethan was seven and Erich was five. They were increasingly more aware of events and curious about our activities. That day, as I put the car into park and turned off the engine, Ethan asked the question I knew was inevitable.

"Why do we come here?" He looked around at the rows of headstones and the trees that lined the road. "Mom? Why do we always stop here?"

I froze for a moment, then I felt a great sense of tenderness. The boys were ready, and Ethan had chosen his own time to receive the information I knew he would want someday.

I said, "Let's walk up to the place we always visit, and I'll explain there." Then, I helped the boys out of the car and walked with them around to the trunk. Retrieving our gifts for Jenny, I asked Ethan to carry the flowers while Erich and I got the candle. The grass was just starting to green, and the buds were blooming on the white dogwood tree behind Jenny's headstone. I noticed the tree had tripled in size since she was buried. The sun shone bright, as it had so many times when we visited her. As we stood in front of the headstone Steve and I had picked out all those years ago, I thought briefly of how our lives had changed since that time of nearly unbearable grief. I felt a wave of gratitude wash over me as I looked at these children, our sons.

Ethan asked if he could place the flowers. He was still holding the pretty pink bouquet, and at my nod, he placed it in front of the headstone. I bent down and carefully set the small glass candle holder on the front rim of the headstone base. I lit the small tealight candle. As I watched the flame start to burn, I reflected back to the day she was born and pictured how perfect and beautiful she was. My sorrow seemed lighter as years passed and Jenny's brothers brought me immeasurable joy, but grief was still simmering deep down inside. We never do "get over it." We never fully "move on."

I recalled reading in college that Sigmund Freud had written a letter to a friend after Sophie Freud, youngest of his daughters, died. After Jenny's death, I looked up that letter and found his words. He had written that the acute sorrow we feel after such a loss will run its course, but also that we will remain inconsolable, and will never find a substitute for the beloved person we have lost. "No matter what may come to take its place, even should it fill that place completely, it yet remains something else. And that is how it should be. It is the only way of perpetuating a love that we do not want to abandon," Freud had declared.

That message stayed with me, and it has brought me some comfort over the years. I often wondered if other parents who had experiences similar to that which Steve and I suffered would find Freud's words helpful. I also thought, as I began to explain our loss to our boys, that maybe our story, too, would someday bring consolation to others.

But, for the moment, I turned my full attention to Ethan and Erich. The question I had always anticipated was now awaiting an answer, and I knew exactly what to say.

I took the boys' hands, pulled them close to me, and said how much I loved them. Then, in the simplest way, I explained that something sad happened before they were born. They realized by my broken voice that what I was about to say was something serious. With my heart full of love, I whispered:

"You have a sister. She is our special angel and her name is Jenny."

Epilogue

I still find it difficult to believe what happened. Perhaps instead of the word "believe," I should use the word "accept." I believe when we find a place of acceptance it allows us to be able to move forward. Some days, I feel that I have accepted the loss of my daughter while, other days, I realize I am not there yet. I carry this sense of loss or that something isn't right within me. My story is deeply personal and private. It's been difficult to write; however, my hope is that it will help others while guiding me to a place of acceptance.

I chose this point in time to write this story as the feelings of loss over baby Jenny have bubbled to the surface. I believe I am having these feelings now because raising the boys has allowed me to keep my emotions at bay all these years. We have had wonderful years together with the busyness of school, sports, and just caring for one another. Now, with Ethan already a sophomore at Hobart and William Smith and Erich heading to Penn State, I am readying for the next chapter of our lives. It seems only natural that these big life changes are opening up feelings of loss again, even though my life's greatest joy has come from raising these two young men.

Over the years, people have asked if I felt bad not having a daughter since I am so close to my mom. A few people have even said I should have tried for a girl. I don't blame those who have said these things. They have not been insensitive, as they have not been aware of my circumstances. But these interactions and the feeling of change as my boys become more independent have created a deep need to speak openly about Jenny.

Today, as I complete this memoir, it's an unseasonably warm March day here in Upstate NY. I am feeling nostalgic. The geese will soon return to usher in a new season as they have every spring. I, too, am preparing for a new season. Time has passed quickly. The boys are grown and ready to fly. Ethan is twenty years old and Erich is eighteen. I am in awe at not only how fast the years have passed, but what amazing young men they have grown to be. It has been a privilege to walk with them on this journey. Time moves on as it always does, and I contemplate this next chapter with mixed emotions. So much has changed, but so much is the same.

I said goodbye to Maude Lilly back in March of 2017. She was 16. On that day she looked at me with those deep brown beagle eyes that had become cloudy over the years and I knew it was time to let her go. And so I did, with gratitude for her unconditional love and companionship over all the years.

We still live in the house where we brought the boys home and have enjoyed it as a place where we have celebrated all our big life moments as a family.

Once a place filled with endless toys and chaos, now a place filled with lighthearted laughs and grown-up conversation. We welcomed a new dog into our lives in the fall of 2017. A sweet mini goldendoodle we named Harriet. We got lucky again.

I often talk about perspective and how life really is all about it. This was baby Jenny's biggest gift to me. She helped me focus not on what I lost that December in 2002, but the perspective that I gained from it. She also taught me that there are no guarantees. It takes just that one moment for everything to change. That is a concept I could never grasp until it happened to me. I know she is with me, just as she and my grandmother wanted me to know when they came to me in my dream all those years ago. I hold on to that. I keep with my tradition and stop at the cemetery anytime I am down in the Binghamton area. And, I always have a bouquet of flowers in hand, a candle to burn bright, and a prayer to lift up. And, at Christmastime, I always place a fresh fir wreath with a big handmade bow on Jenny's stone. It's a tradition never to be broken. A reminder and celebration that I have a daughter, and she is beautiful and perfect.

Made in the USA
Columbia, SC
26 November 2024

47625257R00104